W9-BZC-119

# Unbreakable
# B O N D S

## Practicing the Art of Loving and Being Loved

# Dr. Cheryl Meier
# and Dr. Paul Meier

BakerBooks
Grand Rapids, Michigan

© 2002 by Cheryl Meier and Paul Meier

Published by Baker Books
a division of Baker Publishing Group
P.O. Box 6287, Grand Rapids, MI 49516-6287
www.bakerbooks.com

Second printing, February 2005

Printed in the United States of America

All rights reserved. No part of this publication may be reproduced, stored in a retrieval system, or transmitted in any form or by any means—for example, electronic, photocopy, recording—without the prior written permission of the publisher. The only exception is brief quotations in printed reviews.

Library of Congress Cataloging-in-Publication Data

Meier, Cheryl.
    Unbreakable bonds : practicing the art of loving and being loved / Cheryl Meier and Paul Meier.
        p.    cm.
    Includes bibliographical references.
    ISBN 0-8010-1247-3
    1. Love—Religious aspects—Christianity.  2. God—Love.  3. Spiritual life—Christianity.  I. Meier, Paul D.  II. Title.
    BV4639 .M415  2002
    241′ .4—dc21                                                    2002008436

ISBN 0-8010-6484-8 (pbk.)

Unless otherwise indicated Scripture quotations are taken from the New King James Version. Copyright © 1982 by Thomas Nelson, Inc. Used by permission. All rights reserved.

Scripture quotations marked NIV are taken from the HOLY BIBLE, NEW INTERNATIONAL VERSION®. NIV®. Copyright © 1973, 1978, 1984 by International Bible Society. Used by permission of Zondervan. All rights reserved.

Scripture quotation marked AMP is taken from the Amplified® Bible, Copyright © 1954, 1958, 1962, 1964, 1965, 1987 by The Lockman Foundation. Used by permission.

Scripture quotations marked NLT are taken from the Holy Bible, New Living Translation, copyright © 1996. Used by permission of Tyndale House Publishers, Inc., Wheaton, Illinois 60189. All rights reserved.

Scripture quotations marked NASB are taken from the New American Standard Bible®. Copyright © 1960, 1962, 1963, 1968, 1971, 1972, 1973, 1975, 1977, 1995 by The Lockman Foundation. Used by permission.

To protect their privacy, all names of persons whose stories are shared have been changed, as have their situations.

Unbreakable
# BONDS

I dedicate this book to my husband:
To Aaron, my love, my gentle companion.
You bless my life daily.

Cheryl Meier

David Larson, M.D., psychiatrist and researcher extraordinaire, changed the face of America by bringing true spirituality to science and medical schools across the country (see chapter 9). He died during the writing of this book and was not only one of my closest lifelong friends but my prayer partner. We were psychiatry residents together at Duke in 1974. I dedicate this book to Dave's memory and to his sweet wife, Susan, and two children, Chad (senior at Princeton) and Kristin (senior at Syracuse). See you in heaven, Buddy.

Paul Meier

The more I think it over, the more I feel that there is nothing more truly artistic than to love people.

Vincent van Gogh

# Contents

Foreword     8
Introduction     10

**Part 1 Direction**
1. To Be or Not to Be . . . Loved     15
2. Creating a Path to Love     31
3. Re-membering Yourself     47
4. Determining Your Direction     57

**Part 2 Detection**
5. Cave Sweet Cave     81
6. Am I a Doormat?     96
7. What Do You Expect?     115

**Part 3 Connection**
8. Preparing for Limitless Love     135
9. Practicing the Art of Love     151
10. Connection with Protection     163

**Part 4 Perfection**
11. Changing the Way I Treat Myself     181
12. Creating an Unbreakable Bond with God     197
13. Final Considerations on Your Journey
    toward Love     227

Notes     237

# Foreword

Who doesn't want to be loved and to freely love others? You would think *everyone,* but in my family practice I have cared for many patients who either didn't know how to or chose not to participate in loving, positive relationships—with themselves, others, or their Creator. And I've seen the same phenomenon as I've ministered to many people in and through my church. The causes for broken relationships are many, but all have the potential to be healed. If your soul and relationships are in need of renovation or restoration, this book is just what I (the doctor) order for you.

Starting from the time that Paul and I were together at Duke University in the late 1970s, I have followed his career and writings. The principles of Scripture and relationships that he has taught through the years have penetrated into my spirit and soul and instructed my mind and heart. Now Paul and I are old enough to see the fruit of practicing these truths for almost three decades.

When I learned that Paul and his daughter, Cheryl, had written this book, I not only wanted to read it, but I wanted to read it with my oldest child, Kate. You see, Kate was a recipient of my practice of these ageless precepts. So we read *Unbreakable Bonds* together. After finishing it, Kate wrote: "The way Cheryl writes about her father's unconditional love for her reminds me of the way my dad, in his love for me, points me to Perfect Love, my heavenly Father. Although he has pushed me to excel, despite the fact that I was born with cerebral palsy, Dad has never expected more from me than he thought realistically I was capable of doing and has never condemned me for doing less. He has always supported me, even when I have made a bad decision or mistake. My dad, by learning how to create *unbreakable bonds* with me, has helped me develop *unbreakable bonds* not only with my Father in heaven but with myself and others God has brought into my life."

When all is said and done, we believe that relationships are among the things that matter most. This book will assist you, if you choose, in deepening and improving the meaningful relationships in your life. It will help you repair those that need repair, and it will teach you how to avoid those that might be damaging.

Don't read this book quickly. Invest the time and energy to study it—and yourself. It's an investment that will reap dividends for eternity.

Walt Larimore, M.D.
Kate Larimore

# Introduction

I chose to create this book with my father for the express purpose of uniting people with love. All of us were created to be united with love. In my practice as a psychologist, what saddens me the most is seeing people who are lonely and living without the love in their hearts that was meant to be there. We try so hard to get love through our achievements and in our relationships, yet we become discouraged when we continue to feel unappreciated or unloved. It is ironic that what we need most at such a time is faith and courage to face our deepest fears so that we can approach the love we were meant to have.

To discover real love is to embark on a spiritual quest. We are spiritual beings. Unless we address our spiritual longings for love, the ache will remain in our souls, unidentified and unhealed.

I wholly agree with David G. Benner:

> If psychology replaces religion but does not deal with human spiritual longings or the means for their fulfillment, it replaces it not with some advanced truth, but with a lie.[1]

We do not wish to replace religion. We recognize that all of us have spiritual longings that cannot be satisfied with just "psychological literature" or "biological understanding." Professionally I am a psychologist and my father is a psychiatrist. Personally we are father and daughter, two different generations and two different genders with two distinct views to offer to you on your path to forming deeper love. We created this book utilizing our professional training, education, and experience working with our clients in our respective fields—in clinical psychology and medicine—yet we recognize that this alone does not join people with the love they long for. We both have an education in theology—the study of God—and yet in addition to the "book learning" we offer you our experiences of faith and love in our own lives and the lives of those with whom we have had the privilege of working.

I am drawn to the beauty and wisdom of Mother Teresa's words:

> Holiness is not a luxury for the few; it is not just for some people. It is meant for you and for me and for all of us. It is a simple duty, because if we learn to love, we learn to be holy.[2]

We invite you, whatever your faith, to join us in practicing the art of loving and being loved.

Dr. Cheryl Meier

During my past thirty years as a psychiatrist I have co-authored over fifty books but only one on love. That book was *Love Is a Choice* (Thomas Nelson, 1991), and it struck a nerve. Over a million copies have been sold and it continues to be a best-seller even now. In 1993 on Oprah Winfrey's show, I talked about how unconditional love is a choice and a worthy goal. I also discussed how we can protect ourselves from the "jerks" of this world.

Many changes have occurred in the world since then, including a major attitude shift after the terrorist attacks of 9-11. Human beings across the globe are waking up to the futility of the "rat race" and to the realization that the most important thing we can do to have meaningful lives is to practice the art of loving and being loved. That is the reason my daughter, Dr. Cheryl Meier, and I have coauthored *Unbreakable Bonds*. This book goes into much greater depth than my first one and explains many deep and complicated psychological and spiritual principles of true love. This is not a book to rush through in one sitting. It is a book to digest and ponder in order to understand how these complicated dynamics can be overcome to help you gain access to the wonders of truly loving and being loved, while still protecting yourself from jerks in your past or current environment. Are you ready to take a sometimes painful journey if joy and love are at the other end? If so, let the journey that will change your life begin. Let's roll.

Paul Meier, M.D.

# Part 1

# DIRECTION

What direction am I heading?
Who gave me this direction?
Am I getting what I want by going this way?

# one

# To Be or Not to Be . . . Loved

The ideal is within you, and the obstacle to reaching this ideal is also within you. You already possess all the material from which to create your ideal self.

Thomas Carlyle

We are spiritual beings, created in the image of God. We have been given the gift of a spiritual nature—we are able to love and be loved. We do not merely respond to life based on instinct. God's first action toward humankind was to bless us. His first instruction to us was to make the earth full and be masters of it. Why God gave us this much freedom is a mystery, yet it is ours to search out and understand. It is ours to learn how to become wise masters of this vast domain. In the same way that God gave us this direction to rule the earth, he gave us the ability and freedom to direct our own lives. We can choose to bury this ability and live in reaction to others, to circumstances, or to our instant biological urges instead of consciously choosing to act from the higher place of love. We can choose to disconnect from the spiritual part of our nature and take away the freedom given to us. Or we can choose to respond to this incredible calling and engage in the process of knowing and cultivating our spiritual self. We can then direct ourselves toward love and all that is good.

Though many of us desire deeper relationships with others, we often are resistant to change. Out of our own resistance to the unfamiliar we keep ourselves from the love we want. We may work hard for the approval of others, yet we become disillusioned and disappointed when they reject us or don't give us all the love we are asking for.

It is time we engage in a different approach. Our lives are too precious for us to sit around, hoping and waiting for love to just happen! Our lives are too valuable for us to hold ourselves back, afraid of connection because of past rejection or failures. Our lives are too short for us to hold on to blame and resentment, which keep us stuck, passive, and motionless, unable to get to the destination we desire. Why wait when you have the ability to direct yourself toward love now? When we actively pursue love and consciously work to discover what blocks us from it, we free ourselves and begin to find love in abundance.

With everything going on in our country and our world these days, more and more people realize that now is the time to connect with others. This is what really matters. Now is the time to choose love, to start making a difference in our lives, using our influence and power to transform ourselves instead of investing all our time trying to change those around us. Whatever excuses we have used before, whatever hurdles seemed impassable, now is the time to let them go. In letting go, we invite change and give ourselves the opportunity to forge ahead.

Now is the time to wake up to the possibilities each of us has to add joy and meaning to our daily lives through practicing the art of loving and being loved. We are born with a desire to create unbreakable bonds. This desire motivates us to make the effort to change and engage in a spiritual life of love, a life beyond mere animal instinct. When we truly feel connected with ourselves, with others, and with God, our lives become dynamic, exciting, and inspired.

From the beginning of time people have longed for love. This has been reflected in literature, poetry, and songs. Relationships grounded in love are the essential ingredients to create a meaningful and happy existence. If this is what we want, it is time to discover what is keeping us from fully experiencing deep relationships. We each hold the answer to that question.

One definition of *insanity* is to keep doing the same thing over and over while expecting a different result. A way to protect ourselves from this repetitive madness is to *change* what we are doing so that we can *give ourselves* a different result! This does not mean we randomly change what we are doing and try anything, as long as it is new. This means, instead, we embark on a journey to become consciously aware of

- the direction in which we have been heading
- the reasons we have been heading this way
- the choices we have made to accept this path
- the results we have been experiencing
- how we are accessing our God-given ability to love and be deeply loved

If we're not getting the love we want, we can make changes that will increase our opportunities to discover this love.

When we view our love-ability and connect-ability as an art or a skill that can be developed and matured, we open up ourselves to new opportunities for learning and growing. Rather than getting defensive or self-critical, we can explore the landscape of the relationship skills we now hold and the skills we have yet to acquire.

We have written this book to encourage you in your journey toward genuine happiness. Our intent is to equip you with the skills and tools that will access your God-given ability to love and respond to love. Each of us is given this gift, this artistic ability to love and create. We are able to listen and respond to the truth we find. When we begin to listen to ourselves, we can perceive where disconnections are occurring, how they are affecting us and those around us, and where our unbondedness originates. Our personal pain is calling us not to sit, paralyzed, in desperation but to actively listen to where the disconnection is so that we can respond by connecting with and fulfilling our truest longings to learn the art of love.

## Eliminating the Resistance

As the quote at the beginning of this chapter reveals, you already possess the material from which to create your ideal self. This is a gift from God, whether you do something meaningful with it or not. The quote also reveals a dilemma: The *obstacle* to reaching this ideal is also within you. We can look at it this way:

1. You picked up this book with the desire to increase your ability to love and be loved.
2. You have the desire and the idea of the love you wish to experience, but something is blocking you from taking hold of this ideal love.

It's as though there were opposing forces within you: One force moves you toward your desired experience of love. The other moves you away. As you go through this book, you will most likely be surprised at the amount of resistance you discover within yourself. This resistance keeps you from experiencing ideal love.

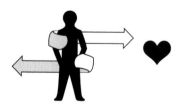

The key to understanding this resistance is in discovering what controls us. As adults we have choices about the direction of our lives. If we choose not to take charge of our life, by default we choose to be led by others. We keep ourselves in a childlike state of dependence. We are free to spend our life getting mad at our parents, getting mad at God, getting mad at our spouse, our children, and our friends for not loving us the way we want to be loved, *or* we can explore what it is to let go of trying to change them and begin investing in changing ourselves. I cannot and do not control God. I cannot control my spouse. I cannot control my children's amount of love for me. I cannot control my friends. I can use my daily energy trying to control all these people and circumstances, or I can begin to direct and inspire *myself* toward deeper loving and connecting.

I can change to

It is amazing to see the results in people when they begin to let go of their inner resistance to love and being loved. Gandhi so profoundly said, "You must be the change you wish to see in this world."

Jesus taught this same concept much earlier when he said, "Take the plank out of your own eye, and then you will see clearly to remove the speck from your brother's eye" (Matt. 7:5 NIV). There is a deep truth to be absorbed in this teaching.

Your initial response may be to balk at this and say, "But you don't know my husband (or wife). If I let my guard down, he'll (she'll) make my life miserable." No one is saying you cannot protect yourself from your husband or whomever else you recognize to be hurtful. You can and you ought to protect yourself; you are worth protecting. But it is also important to recognize that you can protect yourself and still begin to change. You are the only one able to make real changes in your life.

We know how painful it is to wait for someone you care about to turn around and acknowledge your worth and your presence. You just want that person to begin loving you in the way you have always dreamed. But the answer here is not to try to force the person to respond as you desire. As painful as it is, it is important here, in the beginning of this book, to choose to respect the individual freedom of that person. Each person has his or her own personal opportunity to choose love or reject it. If someone close to you chooses to put off pursuing conscious loving, that does not mean you have to put it off in your life. Instead of spending all your energy trying to force them to change, it is essential that you take hold of your personal energy so that you can use it to get through this process of loving and changing yourself. In this way we imitate God's love for us. God does not force his love on us nor does he force us to love him. So also we can learn to practice this art of love with freedom and grace toward ourselves and others.

Again, it is important to remember that you are free to protect yourself. It's okay to avoid potentially painful situations. One analogy that can be useful here is to think of a dog that has a history of biting people. Instead of going into the neighbor's backyard when this dog is in a bad mood and complaining each time the dog bites you, it is important to protect yourself from the dog and stay out of the backyard! That is where the analogy ends, of course, because it is the dog owner's responsibility to make sure people are protected from the dog.

It is possible, of course, for an owner to train the dog. Adult humans, however, are another story. Our training begins in childhood when our parents teach us about relating to others. If an adult chooses not to get further training to change the maladaptive lessons about relationships he or she learned in childhood, then this person may relate to others in destructive ways. In this case, we can set boundaries on our relationship with the person, but we can't force him or her to change. That's up to the individual. Setting boundaries may influence the other person to want to change, yet each person is given the freedom to consider if the cost of changing old patterns is too high. In our legal system this is why we have the protection of jail, which is meant to safeguard society from people who use destructive means to get what they want. The limitations and consequences of jail may also motivate those inside to begin the process of change.

The truth for us is that we do not have to *wait for* misery, divorce, jail, disease, or loss of a loved one to motivate us to have the courage to change and begin loving on a deeper level. Each day we can take every opportunity available to us to increase our training in the art of loving and being loved.

## How Well Do You Connect?

Let's begin with an exercise to explore the direction in which you are currently heading. You will also discover who gave you that direction and how strongly you are invested in staying on this path. With the exercises throughout the book, you will get the best results by being as open and honest with yourself as possible. Suspend the critical and judgmental side of yourself so that you can really begin to get to the core of your innermost thoughts.

### *Exercise 1: Determining the Roots of Your Relationship Skills*

Complete the sentences below:

1. My relationship skills were initially taught to me by: ___
   _____.

2. Three things I appreciate about the relationship skills of this person (these people) are:
   a. _____
   _____
   b. _____
   _____
   c. _____
   _____

3. Three things I wish had been different in the way this person (these people) related to me are:

a. _____

_____

b. _____

_____

c. _____

_____

4. In relationships, my tendency is to:

☐ jump right in
☐ hold back and wait

5. Rate the following descriptive words or phrases from 1 to 5, with 5 meaning this really describes me at this time and 1 meaning this doesn't really describe me right now.

| | | |
|---|---|---|
| Bored ____ | Critical ____ | Stubborn ____ |
| Anxious ____ | Panicked ____ | Tired ____ |
| Dissatisfied ____ | Blah ____ | Unforgiving ____ |
| Depressed ____ | Distant ____ | Helpless ____ |
| Hiding ____ | Disconnected ____ | Empty ____ |
| Addictive ____ | Lost ____ | Fearful ____ |
| Frustrated ____ | Disconnected from | Overworked ____ |
| Full of shame ____ | God ____ | Aggressive ____ |
| Super-busy ____ | Spiritually under- | Sarcastic ____ |
| Drained ____ | nourished ____ | Impatient ____ |
| Have to be neat ____ | Passive ____ | Impulsive ____ |
| Stuck ____ | Confused ____ | Sad ____ |
| Angry ____ | Mad ____ | |

The purpose of this exercise is not for you to beat yourself up. Everyone reading this book has related to several of the above adjectives at one time or another. Honesty is essential here. If we choose not to connect with and understand the areas we struggle in, then we cannot give ourselves the antidote. Also, it is important to keep in mind that when we give ourselves surface answers, we often end up with surface solutions. So do not be afraid to dig for the deeper answers!

Exploring these deeper places within takes time, so remember to pace yourself! It is like trying to lose weight. We get a burst of energy to start working on our physical health. After one day of all vegetables and salads, and after running ten miles with the wrong shoes, it is easy and seems most reasonable to say to ourselves, "Forget this. I'm going back to my old ways!" So also here, give yourself time to discover those deep answers. Pace yourself and understand that your defenses were given to you for a reason. We are learning to let go of our defenses while finding better ways to protect ourselves instead of ripping them away at once.

Our connecting, relational skills were passed down to us by our parents or parent substitutes through their words and actions. Research indicates that up to 85 percent of our personality was formed by age six. Our understanding of relationships came through our early experiences with our parents. We learned how to relate to others by the ways they related to us, around us, and to each other. At five we did not know how to filter, understand, discriminate, and teach ourselves on our own. Being impressionable, we absorbed what we observed in our parents. If Dad was absent, we experienced his absence relationally and emotionally. Often this would translate into a self-message communication—*I did not deserve a father.* If Mom was cold, we learned that moms are distant, and often we imitate that same coldness when we become mothers. If this was the dominant model we experienced, how else can we mother?

We will describe these processes more in the following chapters. Here, we are getting an overview of the areas in our heart that we want to strengthen, and we are beginning to understand the resistance we find within ourselves to carry out this strengthening.

Let's look at your answers in the first exercise. What do they reveal about you?

### Unwrapping the Gift

1. As an adult, I am free to give myself the opportunity to add to and/or let go of the relationship messages given to me by (fill in with answer 1 from exercise 1): _____
   _____.

2. Three ways I am loving to myself and encourage myself toward love are (fill in with answers to question 2 from exercise 1):

   a. _____

   _____

   b. _____

   _____

   c. _____

   _____

3. Three ways I oppose myself on my path toward loving relationships are (fill in with answers to question 3 from exercise 1):

   a. _____

   _____

   b. _____

   _____

   c. _____

   _____

4. When it comes to relationships, my tendency is to (fill in with answer 4 from exercise 1): _____

   A combination of both styles of relating is the best. If we "jump right in," it shows a positive spirit and willingness to pursue a relationship. When we learn how to balance "jump right in" with "holding back and waiting" we teach ourselves thoughtfulness and discretion.

   Generally, if we are the "jump right in" types, the following statements tend to describe us:

   We are overinvested in making a relationship work.
   We cling to the hope that the relationship *will* work this time.
   We may exaggerate (within ourselves and to others) our deep-felt need for connection.
   We may ignore red flags and repeat hurting ourselves in unsafe/destructive relationships.
   We often find distant (hold back) people and try to change them.

We exert effort to open the other person up to relating
more deeply.

We do what we can to get the other person involved in
loving us.

In relation to our parents, spouse, or significant other,
we may still be hoping that they will show up and start
loving us the way we want them to. (Genuine love is
what we seek.)

We most likely bought this book for ourselves or to try to
figure out how to change a distant "other."

If our style is to "hold back and wait," then we tend to
do the following:

We minimize (both inwardly and outwardly) our deep-felt
need for love and connection.

We may miss opportunities because we do not want to
invest in the possibility of feeling rejected again.

We keep ourselves occupied with activities that don't
require very much personal interaction.

We have a proclivity toward group activities, where we can
easily keep emotional issues on a surface level.

We are often drawn to the "jump right in" types, yet their
neediness at times scares us.

We have a deep-felt need for love and intimacy, yet we exert
an extreme amount of effort to deny or minimize our
feelings because we want to protect ourselves from getting hurt over and over again.

We are often detached or aloof in relationships.

In relationship to our parents, often we want them to "jump
right in" to loving us in a healthy and meaningful way.
We feel like we missed out on this in childhood, yet we
say to ourselves, *It doesn't do any good to dwell on it.* We
often describe our childhood as a normal experience,
and yet, by denying our desire for more love/closeness
from our parents, we continue the pattern of withholding from ourselves.

Most likely we were given this book as a gift, or we were
challenged by the thought of deepening our ability to love.

25

5. In question 5 of exercise 1, put a check beside each descriptive word or phrase that you rated 3, 4, or 5. The following list gives those same descriptive words, along with the antidote. The antidote is the positive ideal you can learn to strengthen and work toward. The words you rated 1 or 2 reveal your areas of strength—their antidotes are probably well-developed in you. Consider where you got these strengths and how to build on and fully develop them.

**Bored**—Excited (feel connected)
**Anxious**—At peace
**Dissatisfied**—Satisfied
**Depressed**—Free, joyful
**Hiding**—Accepting
**Addictive**—Temperate
**Frustrated**—Worth filling, full, satisfied
**Full of shame**—Fully acceptable
**Super-busy**—Create time to relax
**Drained**—Replenished
**Have to be neat**—Relaxed, enjoy neatness
**Stuck**—Free to move
**Angry**—Feel protected
**Critical**—Gentle
**Panicked**—Calm
**Blah**—Energized
**Distant**—Able to protect self, initiate intimacy
**Disconnected**—Connected
**Lost**—Embraced
**Disconnected from God**—Honest with God about true feelings
**Spiritually undernourished**—Spiritually fed
**Passive**—I am worth being assertive for, standing up for
**Confused**—Separated, clear
**Mad**—Feel deeply cared for
**Stubborn**—Flexible, kind
**Tired**—Rested
**Unforgiving**—Forgiving, graceful
**Helpless**—Able
**Empty**—Connected with God, self, and others

**Fearful**—Unafraid, courageous
**Overworked**—Balanced
**Aggressive**—Assertive
**Sarcastic**—Protected, kind
**Impatient**—Patient
**Impulsive**—Thoughtful
**Sad**—Full of joy

Take time to think through this exercise, trying to understand what it reveals about you. For example, if you rated "confused" a 5, then you can ask yourself: *Who in my life did not want me to separate, to have my own ideas and thoughts and/or to be my own person?* or *Am I afraid someone is going to reject me or get mad at me if I make a choice that is different from theirs?* To be confused is to be fused with someone or something else. It is to be like Jell-O, unable to stand on your own.

Sometimes when we are confused, we feel like we are in a fog. Think about how difficult it is to drive when it is extremely foggy. So also our lives become more difficult when we continue to side with our fear of separating and making our own choices. Often those of us who are perfectionists, who do not want to get anything wrong, will stay confused so that we do not have to make a choice. We think, *If I choose, I may choose wrong and someone might get mad at me, so I would rather stay confused.*

If you have any other recurring experiences or feelings that weren't included on this list, add them so that you can begin to discover your areas of strength and the areas that need strengthening.

As we have said, many of our feelings and thoughts about ourselves come from "internal messages" instilled by parents and other significant people in our childhood. These feelings, such as being frustrated, miserable, or critical, would not appear to be desirable, but we are rewarded in some way for these behaviors or we would not repeat them. Whatever reward we receive keeps us from finding the antidote.

Often the problem is that we are afraid of change. We think change may make things worse. We have grown comfortable with things the way they are, and we're not willing to put in the effort that change requires. Remind yourself that it is worth it, and you are worth making every effort to love more fully. Even if you do not feel this worth now, you can still choose to treat yourself with respect. As you do, you teach yourself what God intended you to experience in childhood.

## The Way of Healing

One side note before we go on. At times we hear people say, "Psychology is all about blaming your parents," or "Therapy makes people selfish." The word *psychotherapy* is made up of two Greek words, *psyche* and *therapos*, which literally mean "soul healing." There is nothing God wants for us more than that our souls would be healed and truly filled with his love. That healing comes to us in many ways. God has provided many avenues for us to discover his healing love. He wants to free our hearts and souls to truly love. Often the training of a psychologist or a psychiatrist is useful to guide us in fully owning the antidotes to the behaviors that work against us.

Regarding the blaming-your-parents concern, it is important to understand that recognizing where our internal messages came from is different from keeping ourselves in a state of blaming. To recognize where the messages came from helps us realize that they did not originate within ourselves, but instead they were messages that we accepted from others and have often repeated to ourselves in our inner self-talk. To stay in a state of blaming parents or others, refusing to move to forgiveness, is expecting the person who instilled the message in us to show up and change that internal message.

Yes, we were impressionable as children. Yes, we ought to have been protected from unloving messages and experiences that misdirected our sense of self and our learning of relationship skills. We are free to stay mad, and yet in our anger, we remain victims. We wait in a childlike position for the adult to show up and love us instead of embracing our own ability to learn how to love ourselves into adulthood. The only way to move on to

28

wholeness is through the path of forgiveness. For some of us, this is going to be difficult, yet it is essential if we want to fully love and be loved. (There will be more on forgiveness throughout the book.)

Through years of working with people in pain, we have discovered that a central contributor to almost every psychological disorder is this core feeling of disconnectedness or unbondedness. This disconnectedness does not just arbitrarily happen in people's lives. There are reasons for it, and that's what the process of therapy is about. Therapy is similar to the process we are beginning to engage in now, learning to understand where the disconnection started and beginning to reconnect the disconnected parts of ourselves.

If healing comes through connecting, we may wonder why everyone doesn't begin connecting. For some of us, the answer is as simple as not realizing what is possible. For others, the answer is more subtle. We may have a deep fear of being connected because our parents modeled such fear. Without even saying anything, their message to us was loud and clear: "Don't go there—to real intimacy! You *never know* what you will find, or you may be rejected." That message was strong if our parents pushed us away when we were little, trying to get acceptance and affection from them. Nevertheless, we now know we have a choice. We can continue to accept that message or venture out and discover the connection and love we were designed to enjoy.

## Wrapping Up

So far we have introduced and reinforced the following ideas:

Love is ours for the taking, practicing, and developing.
God wants us to be responsible for our lives, but it is our choice to accept that responsibility or give it away.
The internal messages we have believed and followed are learned and have been accepted at some level, at some time, and to some degree.

We have the potential and ability within ourselves to respond to love, receive it, and thus begin the process of becoming our ideal self.

We also have the ability, as adults, to keep ourselves from reaching out to love.

We have the ability to let go of and/or add to the kinds of relationship skills that our parents and others modeled for us.

We have relative strengths and areas that need strengthening within us that were passed down to us, learned from the environment we grew up in, or resulted from the choices we have made. (We also have our genes, which we will discuss later.)

We can spend all of our energy trying to change other people in our lives, blaming them for our brokenness, or we can have the courage to love and change ourselves—and thus become more loving people to those around us!

We can stay the same, wait for something painful to motivate us toward change, or make a free choice to pursue deeper, more intimate love now, the kind that will heal our souls.

Essentially, we can connect with and respond to the longing we have inside to form unbreakable bonds, we can ignore it and leave it undeveloped, or we can keep hoping it grows of its own accord.

Whew! Not a lot of small talk going on here. We have faith that there is love to be found, love that is accessible to all people. We welcome you on this journey and wish to encourage you along the way.

Congratulations! You have completed chapter 1! Commit to yourself and to the process and you will take yourself to the destination you desire. You are worth the challenge!

# two

# Creating a Path to Love

"Now I know," she said, "the further cause of your sickness, and it is a very serious one. You have forgotten your true nature."

Boethius, 523 A.D.

Now that you have made the choice to direct yourself toward love and deeper relationships, it is important to create a path to get there. It is important that you prepare yourself so that you feel safe to travel to a land that is not necessarily familiar to you. Many of us feel anxious when facing the uncertainty and insecurity of visiting a new country, especially when we think we may move there permanently.

You can create an inner sense of safety by beginning to strengthen your ability to be consistent. If you say you are going to show up at a certain time, show up. If you make a commitment to do something, follow through. (It is important to be careful not to overcommit.) Practice being consistent in your speech. As simple as this sounds, practice being honest. Consider a person you know who is almost always late and makes many promises but does not keep them. How safe would you feel traveling to a different country with him or her? In the same way, the more dependable you show yourself to be, the more confidence you will have to let go of your fear and travel to a new land where love abounds.

## So Let's Begin

The first part of our journey begins with a definition. It is important to define the land we come from and also understand something about the land we wish to travel toward. Inwardly you are aware that you want some kind of deeper "love," yet you are probably wondering, *What is love and where can I get it?* Our first ideas of love are formed primarily by the words and actions of our parents. So of course you have a *perfect* idea of love, right?

As loving as your parents may have been, or are now, parents are not perfect. If you want to gain a fuller understanding of love, it is important that you go to a perfect source. If we do not search beyond the model of our parents here on earth, our actions of love will not go beyond the limits of their actions. You *can* stop where they stopped. If they are still searching, wanting to mature their own idea of love, you can follow their example. Regardless of what others or your parents have done or are doing, you have the ability to take hold of a deeper love, invite it into your heart, and by so doing, invite it into the world around you. Your challenge is to discover what your understanding of love is. To do this, ask yourself, *What is love, and where do I find a perfect model of love to invite into my life?*

## What Is Love and Where Do I Find It?

We read in the Scriptures: "Love comes from God. Everyone who loves has been born of God and knows God. . . . God is love" (1 John 4:7–8 NIV). We learn from this:

1. God is love.
2. When you love, you know God.
3. The love you share with yourself and others ultimately comes from God.
4. We know that God is Spirit. He is supernatural. If love comes from God, we know that love is not a natural thing but is supernatural.
5. Thus to access love, we do not pick it from a tree or dig it up from the ground. It is spiritual—it grows in our hearts and comes from God.

So what does this teach us? When I love, I put God's love into action. I engage in a supernatural act from my spirit. In doing this, I know God. God is love, and to be truly loving is to be like God in his very nature. How do I get this love? One way is to remember that I was made in the image of God. God has planted within me, by his grace, the ability to access his love. He created me to form loving relationships with others, with him, and within myself. He does not leave me without the resources to do so.

Our first definition of love, then, is God. The word *define* actually means "to describe an object in its finite nature, or to determine the boundaries of." God is infinite; his boundaries have no end, and so, love is infinite. That is why it is impossible to truly define love or God. Yet we can seek to understand both God and love more, just as we can know our spouse or friends more as we spend time with them.

We know that hate and apathy are the absence of love. We know that heaven is full of love because it is full of God. Hell has been defined as the place in which God is not. One way to think about love is this: To love is to want love to live at its fullest capacity in the heart of each person we encounter; to encourage and not block the true spiritual growth of ourselves and others.

We can *always* learn more about God and about love. Love does not change, but our idea of it can and does change, as we grow in our understanding of it and as we practice it in our everyday life. Another definition of love that helps us understand its nature is this: Love wants every true good for each person in the world. To love yourself, then, is to desire every *true good* for yourself, while simultaneously desiring every *true good* for others.

We know that God wants every true good for each of us, and he knows what the true good is for everyone at all times. We don't always know what the true good is. Our parents could have taught us that our true good was for us to always make them happy, prepare all the meals for the family, keep the house clean, take care of our siblings, and wash all the dishes. Our idea of the true good was thus blurred by the definition we learned through our parents' unrealistic expectations.

We face a challenge here, the challenge of questioning old definitions, understandings, and even our experiences of what we thought was love. If we don't know what love is, how can we direct ourselves toward it? It is possible to gain a more complete understanding of love and thus experience a deeper love within ourselves *if* we are willing to do the following:

1. Commit to fearlessly explore the truths we find in our innermost self.
2. Invite our imagination to expand and enlighten us.

In doing these two things, we give ourselves an opportunity to form loving relationships that last.

There are other ways to find this deeper love, but we chose to teach you this path for two reasons. The first reason is that it works. The second explains the first: This process works because you have ready access to your inner self. You don't have to look for resources elsewhere or pay a lot of money for them. You don't have to wait around for someone else to do what is needed. You use what you already have—the willingness to explore the truths you find in yourself and the imagination to understand them. This is a change from our normal course in life. We know much about our physical selves but seldom take time to know the spiritual part of ourselves. This is where we begin to unlock a true understanding of love.

It is important to recognize that on this inward path you are the only person who can hinder your progress. Consider whether you want to deepen your ability to love and form unbreakable bonds. To go anywhere without fear, even if it is toward a deeper love, it is important to give yourself the freedom to choose that path. This freedom will empower you to accomplish what you set out to do. You are worth this journey. Your life and happiness are worth it. The healing of your soul is worth it. You can choose to commit yourself to this process or you can choose not to. If you do choose to go forward, be gentle with yourself and know that whatever you put into this spiritual journey is what you are going to get out of it and more!

## Finding the Perfect Love

King Solomon, son of David, was known as the wisest person on the earth in his time. The queen of Sheba traveled from the ends of the earth to learn from his wisdom. How surprised she must have been when he revealed to her, "[God] has made everything beautiful in its time. He has also set eternity in the hearts of men" (Eccles. 3:11 NIV). She learned that God has set his truths within the heart of each person. It was certainly worth her long journey to learn this truth. What good was it to her to hold eternal truths within her heart if she did not realize it? Solomon revealed to her that she had had access to these truths all along. She held within herself the potential to discover the deepest truth about love. It is like the story of Dorothy who journeys through all the troubles in the land of Oz only to discover at the end that she had the ability to get home the whole time.

Like the queen of Sheba and Dorothy from Kansas, you have the ability to access the perfect model of love that you are seeking. To discover the perfect nature of love is to understand the eternity God has written on your heart. In A.D. 523 the philosopher Boethius stated a similar truth: "Whatever is learned is a recollection of something forgotten."

If we were born with the knowledge of real love, how can we reconnect ourselves with this knowledge? How can we remember this truth? Why did we forget it? The reality is you have not forgotten this truth completely. As we mentioned earlier, even the fact that you picked up this book points to your desire to increase your capacity for love and unbreakable bonds. Some part of your soul longs to know a love that *lasts* for all eternity. We call these desires *eternal longings*. When we continue with our commitment to fearlessly explore these inner truths and invite our imaginations to shed light on them, we awaken our ability to understand love. Our eternal longings begin to make sense. These eternal longings are universal. We can find traces of them in every culture across time. It is why fairy tales end with "and they lived happily ever after." I am convinced that within our heart of hearts, when we become unashamed to embrace it, we each have the possibility of uncovering our wish to live in the safety of real love forever. We long for a true "happily ever after."

It is ironic that this deep truth that we desire so much can be found in the simplest of ways. J. R. R. Tolkien, Oxford professor and author of *The Lord of the Rings,* wrote an essay on fairy stories, exploring the concept of remembering this truth we once knew. Where some people view fairy stories as stories for children about escaping from reality, he described them as stories for people of all ages, for *recovery* of the highest truths. He wrote that recovery is "a regaining of a clear view . . . seeing things as you are meant to see them."[1]

Recovery of your *self* is the recovery of the essence of who you are and why you are here. Without this essential recovery and understanding of the eternity that is written in our hearts Solomon concluded, "Man cannot find out the work that God makes from beginning and to the end" (Eccles. 3:11b).[2] To truly recover our self is to recover our eternal purpose for being here.

Tolkien encourages us to enrich our concept of love, awaken our imagination, and remember ourselves through reading fairy stories. There is always an antidote to evil in fairy stories. Most often this antidote is an intervention by a form of love or goodness. In these stories we find that even a cinder-girl can recover her recognition that, as poor as she is, she is still remembered and ministered to by someone. She honors the rules set up by her fairy godmother, enjoys her evening, retains one of her glass slippers, and opens up the possibility of freeing herself from the cruelty of her stepmother.

Even though Jack was foolish to buy the "magic" beans when he was starving, he was still able to climb the bean stalk, conquer the unjust giant, and provide for himself and his family.

Pinocchio, a wooden puppet, was given the chance to become a real boy, to love and be loved by his maker, Gepetto. Snow White was hated for her beauty and poisoned by her stepmother, yet she awakened to life again by true love's kiss. There is a reason we are drawn to these stories. Our hearts are warmed when we read the closing words "and they lived happily ever after."

It is when myth becomes truth that we become truly happy. We rejoice when love triumphs over injustice and hate. Your challenge is to equip yourself with the skills and tools necessary to understand the truth about perfect love and awaken this love into the reality of your life.

## Discovering the True Good

You cannot give or receive the love you want until you are able to regain a clear view of what this love is. The word *intimate* comes from the Latin word *intimus*, which means "innermost." According to Webster's dictionary, intimacy is "belonging to or characterizing one's deepest nature." To understand a person is to know him or her. To understand yourself is to take the time to discover who you are. If you wish to draw near to others, it is important that you let go of the fear of drawing near to yourself. When you embrace yourself, you give yourself the confidence to move toward relationships with those around you.

Some of us do not wish to look inside because we are afraid we will find a person who is unworthy of being loved. We wonder, *What if I get to know myself and find a person I don't like?*

But more tragic than this is never getting to know yourself and continuing to reject yourself or the parts of yourself that were rejected in childhood.

If as a child you learned that you are not worthy to be loved, now is your opportunity to recover a clear view. Now is your chance to learn about a truth that is beyond what your parents taught you through their words and actions. The way to do this, as we stated at the beginning of this chapter, is to search out the eternal truths you hold within your heart and engage your imagination to do so. Your communication, thoughts, and actions give you a glimpse, when you attend to them, of the deepest longings in your innermost self. To know these truths is to answer the existential questions philosophers have asked for all time:

Who am I?
Why am I here?
What is my purpose?
What brings me joy and makes my life meaningful?
What is real love?
Do I deserve real love? If yes, why? If no, who said so?

To discover the answers to these questions and the mystery of the eternal truths written on your heart, it is important that you listen. Our ability to silence the pressing world outside and recover our direction, sight, and connection with these truths within us directly correlates with our ability to develop unbreakable bonds.

Some part of us, though it may be deeply buried, remembers that we were created to love and be loved without limit. We each begin in our own sort of Garden of Eden in the calm bliss of the womb. We are brought into this world and begin crying right away to be fed, cared for, and loved. Research has taught us that if infants do not receive human contact and affection, even though they receive sufficient food, they will die. We instinctively begin our quest for affection before we even have a conscious self. We begin to recognize our desire for unbreakable bonds before we are able to read any book on the subject. It is important that you learn to respect this longing you have deep within you and realize it is a natural part of your spiritual journey toward real love.

## Defining Our Earthly Model of Love

Our parents modeled a range of choices for us through how they related to each other, other people, and us. They passed down to us a limited model of love and a limited model of choices, which they had acquired from their parents or learned in life. Unless we consciously seek to expand these models, we act from within the love and choices we have seen and experienced.

For example, suppose when you were a child your parents fed you only ham sandwiches or peanut butter and jelly for lunch. If a friend's mom asked, "What do you kids want for lunch?" you would automatically think she meant, "Do you want ham or peanut butter and jelly?" Similarly, if your parents' model provided you with two ways to cope with problems—cry or run away—then you naturally think those are the only two ways to deal with problems. You continue to believe this until you learn that there are more than two ways to deal with problems. You learn that your choices can be expanded, educated, and enriched.

This is why we emphasize that the essential step toward forming unbreakable bonds is to connect with the eternal truths of God, which he wrote on your heart. By doing this, you consciously choose to expand your choices. Many of us do not realize that we have an expanded range of choices already written on our hearts.[3] As you look to enrich your range of choices by discovering what these eternal truths are, you will begin to offer yourself new options and new meaning. You awaken opportunities that were always available to you.

## Creating a New Model of Choices

Imagine for a moment what you would feel like if someone knew you completely and completely loved you, if every part of you inside and out were fully and wholly loved. If you felt that kind of love, would you still invest the majority of your time and energy running after fame, money, beauty, accomplishment, praise, acceptance, and all of the other things we all pursue to try to make ourselves feel more secure? If you genuinely felt that you were worth being loved without limit, any desire you had to escape from your insecurities—through addictions, food, abuse, unhealthy relationships, proving yourself, staying busy, or zoning out of life—would quickly vanish. If you had access to this limitless love and deeply understood your worth to receive it, you would feel fully loved all the time! You would have an endless source of love to share with others as well.

Whether you have faith that there truly is such a love or not, you can begin expanding your conception of love. Even if you only expand it while reading this book you have the ability to imagine that it is limitless. Imagine that this limitless love can fill you with the love you long for and that access to this love is available to you.

God is infinite, so his love is infinite. Because it is limitless, you can never absorb all the love God has to offer. For the purpose of understanding it in human terms, imagine that you are filled to your capacity and overflowing with the love you long for. This is not about hoping for this love to show up but imagining you have this love now.

We have the ability to access an expanded model of love in our imagination. When we connect with the eternity written on our hearts, we discover that there is no limit to love. So what keeps us feeling insecure and blocks us from actually *experiencing* this love in our lives? This is the dilemma each of us faces. Some of us had truly horrible experiences in childhood in which there was little love. Others of us had a "normal" childhood, yet we still experienced pain or disconnection because our parents were not whole, perfect, or perfectly connected.

If your parents, by their actions and words, modeled to you that you could have only 20 percent of the 100 percent[4] of love available, and no more than 20 percent, then that is what you grew up thinking. Perhaps they had only 20 percent themselves, so they had only 20 percent to give. You cannot give to others what you do not have yourself.

The perplexing situation that we see over and over is people's insistence that their parents were right. They believe that they can have only 20 percent of the available love in the world. We internalize this very deeply in childhood: *If my parents didn't give it to me then it must be my fault. I don't deserve more love than what they gave me.*

Here again is where you can choose to combine your imagination with self-exploration. Let's discover what happens when you accept and live by this 20 percent "truth" that you learned from your parents' model and behaviors:

1. You continually feel like you do not deserve love, like you are not worth more than the 20 percent you were given, so you run yourself into the ground trying to prove your worth to yourself and others (via money, cars, clothes, accomplishments, and living to please others).
2. You may accomplish great things and wonder why you still feel lonely and empty inside after the initial "glow" wears off.
3. You may sabotage your accomplishments or not try at all because you don't feel like you deserve to succeed. You determine that you deserve only to continue trying to get by for the rest of your life with the 20 percent of love you have received.
4. You struggle against your constant feeling of being undernourished in love—unloved and unworthy. You think the only way to solve the emptiness is to fill yourself with alcohol, food, drugs, sex, or other addictions. You use avoidance, anger, anxiety, or needy relationships in efforts to escape. When this doesn't work you feel the pain of the emptiness again. You may reason: *If I am given only 20 percent of love, I might as well find something else to fill this void!* Afterward you feel even more unworthy of love, empty, and full of regret.

You cannot thrive when you are undernourished. It is vital that you challenge yourself to let go of this idea that 20 percent of the love available is all you get. You can keep this model as long as you wish, or you can choose to embrace a different expanded model of love.

You were designed to live on 100 percent of love, and 100 percent of love is available to you. No one has to prove to us that a baby thrives when we give him or her affection and milk. We know we must water our plants and give them sunlight. We willingly care for our pets and feed them. Why then do so many of us fail to remind ourselves of the spiritual truth that *we need love to live?* We can get by with 10 percent, but if 100 percent is available why settle for 10 percent? It is like having a cupboard full of food and allowing ourselves a cracker a day. The love you didn't take hold of yesterday is love that you can use to build on today. If you found a starving person *today,* you would feed the person as much as he or she needed today! In this same way, respond generously with love toward yourself.

Love is available to each person on this earth. Even if you are an atheist and think there is no God, there is still something you can learn about love. If you were the most intelligent and well-read person in the world, consider how little you could read in your whole lifetime compared to what is available. Even if you knew all the languages of the world, there would still be so much information you had not yet come across that you could hardly measure the amount.[5] It is possible that the truths that God formed you, created you in his image, created you to be loved, and loves you have not yet entered into your realm of information or experience.

Those of us who experienced .001 percent of love growing up may find it hard to imagine the possibility of a God who made us and loves us! Nevertheless, not acknowledging God does not make him stop existing. In the same way, if this love truly is available, not acknowledging it does not mean it doesn't exist. It simply means it does not yet exist for you. You have not yet taken hold of it.

In our work as a psychologist and a psychiatrist, we see people who sincerely love God and yet still feel distant from him, as though he has only 10 percent of love to give them. The other 90 percent of their experience is condemnation, guilt, expectations, and all sorts of things that we project onto our understanding of God. When people say things to these 10 percent–thinkers such as, "God loves you," there is an automatic translation in their mind: *Sure, God loves me with this 10 percent, just like I experienced from my earthly father and mother.* Whether we experience God's love, our own love, or the love of others at 5 percent or at 95 percent, we all have room for growth in our hearts. The good news is that there is love available for the taking.

When we insist on keeping the percentage under 100 percent, we leave ourselves underloved. We do this for many reasons, the most common being:

- If I let go of this 10 percent to embrace something else, I may have nothing.
- I was taught that I do not deserve more.
- I am not good enough to deserve more.
- I do not want to change anything; I am scared of change.
- This percentage of love is all I know.
- My parents are good people. If more love were out there, they would have given it to me.
- I cannot have more love than my parents have. How presumptuous is that?
- Even though I am an adult, I am afraid my parents will get mad at me for going beyond the limits they gave me.

Remember what you discovered in the last chapter. As a child you did not yet have the tools to filter what was being taught to you. You did not yet have discernment. You translated your parents' actions as you experienced them. As an adult you now have a choice whether you want to keep living by that same message—you deserve only 20 percent of the love you were made to live on—or you can choose to experience the fullness of the love you were meant to have.

I (Cheryl) remember vividly as a teenager being so mad at my dad because he said, "I love you unconditionally, Cheryl."

And yet, as much as he tried, his love was full of more conditions than I could count! I couldn't define it then, yet I saw how much more praise and attention I would get than my brothers or sister when I got good grades in school and excelled in extracurricular activities. I did not want to be rejected, so I continued to achieve until I burned myself out. As much as my dad wanted to love us equally, it sometimes felt like his pride was damaged when we didn't measure up to his expectations. He seemed to feel better about himself when we excelled. So I felt pressure to succeed. If I failed, it would affect Dad's sense of worth. It was a lot of pressure to be in charge of my parent's self-worth! I soon found myself thinking that I had to "do good" to make God like me more—and to make God feel better about himself (as if God, who *is* love, needs us to make him feel better)!

My father recognizes this "unspoken pressure" now because he knows that he *did* have conditions. He had a strict German father who spanked him if he used scissors on the Sabbath. If he got five *A*s and one *B+* on a report card, his father would ask him why he got the *B+*. My father was in his twenties when I was a little girl, and he had not yet worked through all of the conditions (withholding of love) he still placed on himself. He was very hard on himself, following his father's pattern. Of course he had conditions on his love for me, as much as he intended to be unconditionally loving to each of his children.

Again, you cannot give to others what you have not yet experienced and do not have within yourself. I was mad as a teenager because I read in the Scriptures that God loves us and that his love is unconditional through Christ who met all of God's conditions in the law. I understood that grace was available to me, yet I thought, *I am never going to measure up to God's "unconditional" love if I cannot measure up to my dad's!*

We often think that unconditional love means accepting every choice, word, or behavior from a person. This is why parents sometimes think that if they discipline their children, they are teaching them that their love is conditional. The word *discipline* means to teach or learn; it comes from the word *pupil*. As adults our whole spiritual journey toward love and happiness is to learn what "the true good" is for ourselves and offer it to others. As parents it is our responsibility to teach our kids how to choose "the true good," what is ultimately best for them, so that when they are adults, they will see clearly what the true good is. Until they are about fourteen (even after that sometimes), they will think that staying up all night and eating doughnuts for every meal is the true good. Allowing them to stay up all night every night is clearly not practicing unconditional love. They will not know better unless we train them, by our own actions and the guidelines we give them.

God disciplines us because he loves us, not, as we sometimes think, because he doesn't love us. If he did not love us, he would not bother to teach us and free us from self-destruction. As we engage in the effort it takes to love our children, we love and discipline them to make them more lovable.[6] Applying this process to our spouse and neighbor is another story!

All of us have much to learn about unconditional love. This is why my father and I encourage you to join us in learning to access this unconditional love for yourself and for others, and to tell your kids that you are not perfect at it!

The legalistic years I went through as a teen were difficult. I thought I had to be perfect or else God would not love me, even though I knew, from the Scriptures, that the truth was otherwise. Children are concrete in their understanding. They hear Dad say, "I love you." Mom says, "I love you." Both parents say, "God loves you." So why would a child think that God's love is bigger than the love that parents demonstrate?

We have the ability to hold on to a truth that is real and deeper than the messages from our earthly parents. As simple as this may sound, we often do not think about this. The truth found in God is higher than the truth of our parents. God's love is greater than whatever percentage of love our parents can give. "May your unfailing love be my comfort," writes the psalmist (Ps. 119:76 NIV). God's love is unfailing and limitless. It endures forever.

When we are adults, we alone are responsible for not getting to know this deeper love. We don't do it on purpose; there are reasons why we keep the love out, why we imprison ourselves or keep our spiritual self undernourished. Just because there are reasons, however, does not mean they are reasonable! As G. K. Chesterton so aptly put it: "Madness may be defined as using mental activity so as to reach mental helplessness."[7]

It is important that you consciously make time now to connect with these eternal longings and explore the mystery of the eternity written on your heart. It is time to direct your mental and spiritual energy into inviting more love in. (We will explore how to do this in the next chapter.)

# three

# Re-membering Yourself

We are the music makers and we are the dreamers of dreams.

Willy Wonka

If you want to be wholly loved, you must begin by becoming whole. I laughed in delight when this concept was first introduced to me by a wise man named Dr. Allen Surkis. He said, "To remember our wholeness is to re-member ourselves." In essence, re-membering our wholeness is putting ourselves back together again like Humpty Dumpty so desperately needed! Re-membering ourselves is a process of placing our disconnected members or scattered selves back together into their original wholeness. Essentially this process is about piecing back together the parts of ourselves that were rejected in childhood. In re-membering yourself, you learn to reintegrate and accept the parts of yourself that you were told were useless, bad, or socially unacceptable.

This process of re-membering takes conscious effort. When you re-member, you become whole again. You regain your balance and focus. You recognize that your personality is multifaceted. You move beyond performance, achievements,

47

or problems and embrace your own inward, whole, dynamic self.

We are often distracted by our own pain or immobile because we are still waiting for our parents to come and heal us. Our wholeness comes, however, not from waiting but from remembering what was forgotten, attending to the part of ourselves that the pain is pointing us to. Once we find that part, we are able to begin the process of healing. Pain always indicates that some part of us longs for healing. You can be afraid of pain, you can perpetuate pain, or you can listen to your pain and invite love and healing.

Dorothy, an orphan living with her Auntie Em, dreamed of a land over the rainbow, where she was not in the way, where people loved her, and where her dreams could come true. When she got to that land, she found that all the love she needed had been available all along. All she had to do was take hold of it.

When you read a promise of God in the Psalms, how do you process it in your mind? "Delight yourself in the LORD and he will give you the desires of your heart" (Ps. 37:4 NIV). Do we read that to mean "only one desire" or "just a few" or "more than we can possibly imagine"? We often twist the words to fit in with the model we already have in our mind. Our parents gave us 20 percent; therefore God will too. Instead, we can invite the Scripture to expand our thinking—from 20 percent of the love we see to the 100 percent of love available, from 10 percent of the sincerity we think is in his words to the 100 percent sincerity that he has when he says them. How odd that we look to so many places for help, when the promises of God are so readily available. If God is truly the creator of the universe, then surely there could be no richer and more complete model of choices than found in his Word!

There is order in the universe waiting to be re-membered. The story of Adam and Eve reveals how brokenness and disorder came into this world. The apostle Paul says that even the earth that God created longs to be restored, to live happily ever after!

For we know that the whole creation groans and labors with birth pangs together until now. Not only that, but we also who have the firstfruits of the Spirit, even we ourselves groan within ourselves, eagerly waiting for the adoption, the redemption of our body.

Romans 8:22–23

We see in nature glimpses of the order that exists: Day follows night; the seasons follow their yearly pattern; the moon follows its monthly cycle. This same order, which we find in each atom and each strand of DNA, exists within our souls. Jesus, when teaching us to pray, encouraged us to invite the love and order that is already real and alive in heaven to be fulfilled within us now and in the world around us: "Our Father. . . . Your will be done on earth as it is in heaven. Give us this day our daily bread" (Matt. 6:9–11).

In the same way that you invite God's order to be here on earth, you can invite his love and order to be in your life on a daily basis. You can invite God to give you wisdom in recovering a clear view, in expanding your percentage of experience of the love available to you, and in re-membering the parts of yourself that were never meant to be rejected!

It is important to be gentle with yourself in this process. Your spiritual self is like your physical self in that just because you read about a great workout in a magazine and want to do it, you won't have ten years' worth of results overnight. How exciting it is, though, that you are on the path toward genuinely making a difference in your life! You are walking toward love and expanding your understanding of what real love is.

All of your experiences in life can be utilized and transformed in this process of learning how to truly connect. Connecting involves awakening your senses to the underlying longings concealed within yourself. Our five senses have been aptly described by Leonardo da Vinci as "ministers of the soul." When we forget that we have five senses—or they have become dull from disuse—we miss out on nourishing our emotional selves.

We can describe an ocean to someone who has never seen one, but only the actual experience of feeling oneself swept up

49

by the ocean's waves and becoming part of something incomprehensibly powerful can change one's life forever. To awaken and expand your perceptions, you must be wholly in these places and reflect firsthand on your experiences. It is through treating yourself in a more loving way and accessing the limitless love available to you that you create a new set of "familiar" experiences. In re-membering yourself, you teach yourself that it is safe to go to the areas you have not explored within yourself for years!

We are adults who can begin to think as adults and feel the safety and security of forming an inner awareness that is full, rich, and alive. We can walk without fear toward the love we long to experience through connecting with ourself, with others, and with God. We can open our hearts to the love and to the loving guidance offered to us on our journey toward wholeness.

Whether you are married or single, eighty-five or eighteen, you can begin this process of re-membering yourself and by so doing begin the process of seeing others as they truly are. You can begin your own journey toward building a foundation for intimacy.

## Ten Exercises for Re-membering Yourself

This book is a springboard. We provide exercises for you to do now and also return to and do over and over as you grow. You can also create your own exercises or modify ours so that they more closely fit who you are.

1. Remember your favorite quote or story, or your favorite part in a book you read recently or in a play or a movie. Recall something to which you had an inward response. (It works best if you do not filter through many responses but go with the first one you think of and see what happens!) Write out the phrase or describe the scene. Consider what part of yourself this quote or scene is speaking to. The story may remind you of something funny or it may unearth some pain within you. Write your thoughts in a notebook. Describe what parts of yourself the

quote seems to draw out. What thoughts, feelings, or understandings are awakened by your encounter with the scene you chose? (If you do not want to take the time to write these things, say them aloud during your commute to work or think them to yourself on the subway.)

2. Remember one of your most pleasant memories from childhood. Recall as much of it as possible. Where were you? Describe the sounds, smells, tastes, and textures. Try to feel the joy you experienced then. No matter how old you are now, as Madeleine L'Engle so beautifully reminds us in her book *Walking on Water* (Shaw), you are still two years old, and three, and twelve, and sixteen. Even if you are eighty-five now, it does not cancel out the reality of those earlier ages, with all the experiences and sensations stored away from those earlier years.

3. Many of you may have felt unprotected during your childhood. You may have felt criticized or rejected, as all of us do at some point, especially when going through junior high and high school. It is important to see yourself now as an adult who is learning how to re-member and protect yourself.

Place yourself in one of those experiences (not a highly traumatic one), and see yourself as you are now, standing next to yourself as a child. Protect yourself as a child. Take yourself out of the situation, or be a loving mother, father, or friend to yourself within that situation. Teach yourself now what you wish you had been taught then. Encourage and affirm the reality of your worth and meaning that you were not aware of then.

For my clients who have a relationship with God, or who are seeking one, I ask them to imagine God as they know him now. Give God a human form if you wish. See him with you in the midst of whatever was going on. Know that he sees the brokenness. (Be careful not to assume that your heavenly Father is like your earthly father or mother. Research indicates that most people view God as a supernatural projection of their earthly father and/or mother.)[1] Entertain the possibility that God is more loving than the most loving parents you can imagine. God does not justify any of the words or actions of others that did not come from love. He recognizes them as broken, not what he intended. He wants you to invite him to join you, and he will protect you now so that you can begin the process of reclaiming your *self*, which was lost and hurt by this experience. You were not destroyed, for you are here now, alive. God does not want that part of you to be destroyed.

If you did not get to experience life as a seven-year-old because your parents were going through a divorce when you were seven, this is your opportunity to revisit age seven. Begin to be kind and gentle so that the seven-year-old can be alive within you now, along with the eight-year-old, the fourteen-year-old, and so on.

4. Think of a hobby you never got to do as a child or teen. Create a way to do it, even if it is just for a few hours or one day. Sketch a scene, build a model train, plant seeds in a flowerpot, sign up for one guitar lesson, check out a foreign language tape from your library and work on it for a day, take a tap dancing or ballet class, or go to a park and play a game of basketball. Imagine yourself on the team you wanted to play with. Give yourself a taste of this experience now.

5. Our sense of smell is said to be the strongest of all the senses for helping us recall past events. Remember a smell you enjoyed at any point in your life. Describe it. Is it sweet, strong, mild? Is it a floral scent, a fruity scent? Actually find something with that scent and smell it again if you can. What memories does it recall?

Let your sense of smell relax you. Light a scented candle. Treat yourself to a scented bubble bath.

6. Remember a song you heard when you were younger or one you have connected with recently. Play that music while you are doing your hobby, making dinner, or doing nothing but listening. Hear the different sounds, melodies, harmonies, rhythm, instruments, voices. Make the effort to go to a live show and focus on the creativity of the musicians playing. Be aware of how they each listen to the other instruments intuitively, or how the chords of the guitar seem to listen to one another, interweaving sounds in harmony and wholeness. Allow your mind to engage with the music and freely see the images that come to your mind.

7. Remember a taste you experienced as a child, something that was a treat for you. You may not have tasted this flavor for a long time. Whether it was cinnamon toast, a grilled cheese sandwich, or bubble gum ice cream, remember the taste. If you can find the food or make it, do so. Share it with your children, spouse, or friends.

8. Remember your body. Exercise, walk, stretch, or swing on a swing. Having full use of your body is a wonderful gift. Be aware that not everyone has this gift. If you are able, run, swim, walk up a hill and down a hill. Movement of your body encourages movement within and releases pleasurable endorphins. Balancing on one leg can awaken an inner understanding of where imbalance is or simply how it feels or affects the rest of your body. Know your body's capacities and limits. Learn how it feels to increase stamina, balance, and flexibility.

9. Remember to notice the environment around you—the air, trees, stars, sounds, sunrise, and sunset. Drive to a place you consider beautiful. Go to the zoo and watch the animals playing. Think about a place you do not necessarily consider beautiful in its appearance, yet it is your favorite place to be. Describe what makes it beautiful to you. Open your eyes to the beauty that is continually around you. Consider the uniqueness of each city, bus stop, or tree you encounter.

10. The last remembering exercise is an exercise of remembering the homeless, hungry, broken, widowed, elderly, orphaned, lonely, wealthy, and crippled people in your neighborhood. Remember those in the city in which you live, in your country, in nearby countries, and those in the countries farthest away from you. Choose a whole day to be mindful of them, conscious that they have names. Each motherless and fatherless child is facing another day again, wherever he or she is.

Remember those who are locked in prison either justly or unjustly. Most are imprisoned for the destructiveness they caused against others. Remember, for we ourselves are like them when we imprison ourselves by enslaving ourselves to whatever is not of love. Our imprisonment also affects others. Remember that many who are in prison experience mental illness, loneliness, pain, and brokenness.

Remember those who have been married and widowed. They carry within them a lifetime of memories of another who is no longer in their presence. Divorce can be even more painful for some. Remember with love those who have gone through the rejection of divorce, and also remember their children.

Remember those who do not have a home, a place of refuge to return to away from the struggles of the world. Remember those who have no money or resources to provide food for themselves or their children. Remember to love them, protecting them when it is within your ability.

Remember those who are unemployed or those who have trained for a profession that is not currently in demand. Remember their pain in their insecurity and fear of being unable to survive. Remember them with love and courage, for you do not know if or when you will experience this same need.

Remember the artists, actors, and musicians who bring so much music, beauty, and richness into our lives. Some of them, after years of practice, can hardly make a living from their gifts and talents.

Remember those who are physically or mentally challenged. Picture in your mind those you have met or know personally. Remember those who are in the hospital with an injury or illness. Take time to visit or send them a card. Be mindful that for some each breath is a struggle or each step causes strain on their joints. Remember that they are beautiful and are here for a reason. They have a tremendous amount of life within them just waiting to be awakened!

Remember the elderly. Many have lost their mobility and have lost their dearest friends in life. Do not fear being with them in their joys and grief. They are not dead. It is important to include them in our lives.

Remember the individual people and families in the world who live in countries that are at war. Pray for them. Also sow peace and love toward the stranger and foreigner who lives in your town. Remember those who are oppressed. Be aware of what your country is doing for these people.

There is a psalm that reminds us to "pray for the peace of Jerusalem" (122:6). I have so often done this and not thought about why. Jerusalem is the "city of the great King." Presently, all religions coexist in the city of Jerusalem. This is the city where Jewish, Muslim, and Christian tradition teaches that the Messiah will return in the end times.[2] Remember the places you have lived. Pray for peace for those who live there and for people in other places you have visited.

Remember the wealthy people you know or have heard of with love in your heart toward them. We do not know if love is alive in their hearts, and we want this love for all people. This love is the true water of life, limitless and full of grace. Remember these wealthy people, for they may be lost, lonely, without a clue as to how to acquire true riches and abundance in their life. In most major cities, the wealthiest areas have the highest suicide rates. Have compassion on those who are rich in money but poor in love.

Remember those you have known who have passed on. Recall the love and beauty they brought to this world or a quality you remember about them. Remember the part of you that was drawn out when you were in their presence. Remember their smile. Forgive yourself for any harm you may have caused them. Forgive them for any harm they caused you. Remember their love.

Remember the mothers and fathers who have lost a child or who are unable to have one. Remember their loss and choose not to be afraid of their grief. Remember them with love. Remember also those who have had abortions and think about the lives that were lost through those abortions. Remember the aborted child with love. Remember the mother and father with grace.

Remember the broken people within this world, for we are all broken in some area. Remember those all around the world who are recovering from some kind of addiction that held them captive. Remember them with patience and choose to be patient with yourself, not giving yourself excuses but offering yourself love.

Remember that you are not alone in this universe. These are all your brothers and sisters, your mothers and grandmothers, fathers and grandfathers, sons and daughters. When we do not remember others, it's the same as forgetting ourselves. Our growth is stunted and love is blocked out of the empty places where love wants to enter.

Encourage yourself to set out on the path toward wholeness. Each day has a new dawn. Remember the person you long to be and love him or her into existence.

# four

# Determining Your Direction

Man is obviously made to think. It is his whole dignity and his whole merit; and his whole duty is to think as he ought. Now the order of thought is to begin with self and with its Author and with its end.

Blaise Pascal

For intimate relationships to be securely formed, it is important to build on a strong foundation. In chapter 1 you asked yourself: Do I want to love and be loved? In chapters 2 and 3 you committed to the process of exploring the truth within yourself, using your imagination, and in so doing, expanding your model of love and recovering your wholeness. The third step is to choose to take an active role in your own life, to choose to move in the direction you desire. The more you work on the foundation you began in chapters 1, 2, and 3, the more equipped you are to make good use of the information in the rest of this book.

### Inviting Wisdom to Join You

The key to making choices comes through separating yourself from your parents. Just as in chapters 2 and 3 you invited your imagination to expand your awareness of choices, so in this chapter we invite *wisdom* to inform our choices and priorities. Before you go on, take a moment to reflect on or even to memorize the truths about wisdom found in Proverbs 3 (NIV):

1. "Blessed is the man who finds wisdom, the man who gains understanding, for she is more profitable than silver and yields better returns than gold."
2. "She is more precious than rubies; nothing you desire can compare with her."
3. "Long life is in her right hand; in her left hand are riches and honor."
4. "Her ways are pleasant ways, and all her paths are peace."
5. "She is a tree of life to those who embrace her."
6. "Those who lay hold of her will be blessed."

You are blessed if you find wisdom. She gives you long life, honor, and true riches, the kind of riches that no one can take away from you. Wisdom is more precious than rubies, more profitable than silver. You get more back from wisdom than you would from gold, and nothing that you desire can compare with wisdom. The path of wisdom is a pleasant path, and on it you are at peace. She is a tree of life to you when you embrace what wisdom wants to teach you. On top of all of that, this same chapter teaches us: "By wisdom the LORD laid the earth's foundations, by understanding he set the heavens in place" (v. 19 NIV).

God accessed his own wisdom before he laid the foundation of the universe. It is a good thing too! I have read that if the earth were tilted three degrees in a different direction, we would all burn from the sun's heat.

So how are you to access God's wisdom? In the New Testament James teaches us that we can acquire wisdom by asking God: "If any of you lacks wisdom, let him ask from God, who gives freely and with no reproach, and it will be given to him. But let him ask in faith, doubting nothing" (James 1:5–6).[1]

Isn't it crazy that we have access to the same wisdom that God used to lay the foundations of the earth and we have not yet asked for it? God wants to freely give you this wisdom, but he does not force it on you. He waits for you to take hold of what he freely offers.

## Making an Active Choice

When you make choices as an adult, you are no longer passively led, as a child. You set yourself on a path of acquiring the skills and tools necessary to guide your mind, emotions, and soul toward that which is good and true, toward that which will ultimately make you happy.

On this active path you discover there are more possibilities available than you have ever imagined before. You now have more choices than the ones passed down to you by your parents. In this freedom, you give yourself the room to grow and expand, to travel into unexplored areas and lost places in the world around you and within you.

This chapter is entitled "Determining Your Direction" because we find that if you do not consciously choose to direct yourself with wisdom, you will inevitably become confused and lack purpose. To access your ability to make choices, it is essential that you choose to be your own person. I know, you are probably thinking, *I already am my own person.* If you are, fantastic! This will just be review for you. If you are not, you will learn in this chapter about the hidden ways you let other people direct your life. You will learn how to take hold of your own life and your own purpose, instead of passively waiting for someone else to direct you. If you lead the way, others are free to follow you, but you ultimately make the choices about where it is you are going.

## Separating from Our Parents

So often people come in for therapy and say, "I feel stuck. I don't know what I want to do with my life. I'm confused." The psychological understanding of the word *confusion* refers to "blurred boundaries": *con* means "with," *fusion* means "fusing or melting." When you fuse or melt your boundaries with those of someone else, you become confused; you no longer identify a clear sense of self, purpose, or direction. In fact, the archaic definition of the word *confusion* is "to lead to ruin" or "to throw off the path."

Proverbs tells us over and over to seek out the straight paths and acquire wisdom, or we will lead ourselves to destruction. "Ponder the path of your feet, and let all your ways be established" (Prov. 4:26). In the Book of Hebrews we are encouraged to make our paths straight so that we do not disable ourselves: "Make straight paths for your feet, so that what is lame may not be dislocated, but rather be healed. Pursue peace with all people, and holiness" (12:13–14). When you remain in a confused (melted together), ambivalent, and passive state, you inadvertently lead yourself to ruin and block your own path to wholeness and happiness.

This is why it is important to stop and attend to where the "melting" is occurring, so that you can move from confusion into clarity. When you are in tune with yourself and heeding the messages you communicate to yourself, you will find that your confusion is telling you three things it wants: identity, separation, and clarity. Confusion indicates that you are blurring your boundaries with someone else, whether it is your spouse, your parents, your children, God, your coworkers, or society. We all face the inevitable separation at birth from the warmth and security of the womb to the cold fluorescent lights of the hospital room. The cord is cut between your mother and you; you are separate beings, yet you are utterly dependent on your parents to provide for your needs. The physical separation begins here, yet the emotional/spiritual separation comes only through a lifetime of development.

*Separation* is defined as "being distinct, set apart, disconnected or severed." At birth the umbilical cord is severed. We sometimes wish the emotional separation were just as clear and easy. It is your challenge here to gain wisdom and understanding about how to progress through this process.

The first important concept for us to understand is the *distinction* or difference between a *child* and an *adult*. Separation into adulthood is a lengthy process through developmental stages in which many of us get stuck. This may seem basic to you, yet it is essential to understand in order to create a secure foundation for moving forward.

Let's think about the child:

- A child is dependent on his parents for everything.
- A child's sense of self-worth, identity, and belonging comes almost completely from her parents' words and behavior.
- A child will *die* unless his parents hold, nurture, and provide for him.
- A child forms an understanding of the world by the world she sees around her, how her parents relate to each other and to her. For example, if a boy's father leaves him and his mother at an early age, he will naturally think: *What have I done wrong to make my father leave me? What is wrong with me to cause him to leave? What am I worth if my father chose to throw me away? What are women worth if my dad chose to throw my mom away?* A young girl thinks: *What am I worth as a discarded child? When I grow up, will a man do this to me? Am I worth more than my mom? Will a man keep me?*

Now let's look at the adult:

- The adult creates and develops his own identity (creates identity with a conscious purpose, connected to eternal truths, with the aid of imagination and wisdom from God).
- The adult is independent from her parents and interdependent on others.

- The adult is able to nurture and provide for himself.
- The adult is able to form meaningful relationships with people.
- The adult forms an understanding of the world by what she allows to enter her environment via work, society, church, friends, books and knowledge, movies and entertainment, and so on.
- The adult understands the nature and reality of what he experienced in childhood and learns how to let go of false assumptions and beliefs handed down from parents.
- The adult has the ability to be consciously proactive in forming an identity based on truth.
- The adult takes charge of her own spiritual, emotional, and physical well-being.

Basically, an adult has the ability to be active, to take hold of his or her direction, and to love and nurture self. A child does not have this ability. A child is utterly dependent and passive and waits in hope that his or her parents or parent substitutes will show up and provide care.

Babies do not even understand that their mom is a distinct other, separate from themselves. Psychological research shows us that most babies think that when their mother leaves the room, a part of them is leaving the room. That is why they cry. Some researchers also suggest that we do not discover we are separate from our mother until we are at least eighteen months old.

The reality is some of us have *never* truly separated emotionally from our mother and father. Some parents, whether this is a conscious or subconscious choice, encourage continued dependency because of the feeling of power it gives them. They derive their sense of significance and worth through controlling another human life. A child can stay dependent on his or her mother or father, even into adulthood, because he or she is afraid to become a separate person and/or fears parental rejection.

Without a separate self, there are no individual choices. If I were still a part of my mother, she would be making the choices for me. Or I would be fighting her to make choices for both of us, and she would not be a separate self. The beauty is, when we learn what it is to be separate and whole, the fight does not have to occur.

Separation is not an automatic process. To adopt an adult role distinctly separate from the child role requires conscious effort. It is no surprise, then, that scholars indicate that separation is one of the key elements of holiness. We discover in Adin Steinsaltz's translated writings: "The root meaning of the concept of 'the holy' in the holy language [the Hebrew Scriptures] is *separation:* it implies the apartness and remoteness of something . . . to be holy is, in essence, to be distinctly other."[2]

God is clearly distinct from us in his infinite nature, and thus holy in infinite ways. The Scriptures remind us that each of us is a different part of the body, which forms the church. Each of us has our own talents and gifts with a distinct and separate role. George MacDonald so beautifully captures our separateness in his *Unspoken Sermons:*

> How shall the rose, the glowing heart of the summer heats, rejoice against the snowdrop risen with hanging head from the white bosom of the snow? Both are God's thoughts; both are dear to him; both are needful to the completeness of his earth and the revelation of himself.[3]

To accept and embrace our separateness is to embrace the holiness within ourselves. In this way, again, we reflect the image of God in which we were made. To embrace our own separateness is to appreciate the unique beauty and individuality each person on this earth has hidden within.

### When Separation Is Inhibited

For deep intimacy and connection to take place, the two people must be distinct and separate. In the course of our work as a psychologist and a psychiatrist, we find that many problems are formed because healthy separation has not yet taken place. In some cases children were beaten if they tried to be separate.

Imagine if a parent is insecure about his own education and his child comes home wanting to share the new things she learned in school that day. Out of his own feelings of insecurity, the father gets angry at his daughter for "making him look stupid." Really, all she wanted was someone to be proud of her. She was independently learning new things and was excited to share her new knowledge.

It is often the case that the parents who are afraid of their own separateness are the ones who react so adversely to the separation of their children. They feel threatened by separateness because it is something they have not given themselves. A distinct sense of *otherness* is unknown to these parents. The idea of separateness seems too unpredictable to them, so they try to shut down this process of separation or punish their children for becoming adult others.

When this separation does not take place, our lives are on hold. We often remain in a "confused" state because we think we are going to offend the person we are fused with. By making an active or conscious choice, we are "risking" offending our spouse, parents, coworkers, or children. When we choose to stay fused, because we don't want to rock the boat, we add to our own feelings of inadequacy, rejection, confusion, ambivalence, and lack of direction or focus. We act out of the passive side of ourselves and give away our opportunity to be a distinct and separate other. We shut down our own thoughts and ideas because we don't want to offend. At the core we are afraid of losing the "love" of others. We diminish ourselves because we would rather keep them around. We take away our own power and abdicate our ability to choose and direct ourselves.

One of the strongest pictures I have of this dynamic comes from the book *My Name Is Asher Lev* by Chaim Potok. Asher Lev is an artist who was born into a strict Orthodox Jewish family. He tries to form his own individuality and separateness by developing his artistic ability. His father finds him drawing sketches and becomes angry at him for wasting his time doing something so silly and useless. Throughout the story you see Asher's own inner pain and struggle of being rejected by his father, yet he continues on to develop and cultivate his individual identity and become a separate other.

This theme is familiar in clinical work. Some parents have a box into which their child must fit. A healthy parent, on the other hand, will discipline the child and teach him or her to form a loving character, while allowing the child to develop his or her own unique gifts and abilities. There is not *one* mold that all the children in a family must fit into. This may mean that not all the boys in the family want to be on the football team!

A coach knows that he cannot train each of his Olympic athletes with the same techniques and strategies. As little children we are taught that no two snowflakes are alike. No leaves, no fingerprints, no two DNA strands are exactly alike. So why do schools, parents, or churches often try to make children all the same, squishing them into the same little boxes?

This is a good student box.
This is a devout religious box.
Here is a good worker box.
Here is a good child box.
This is a good listener box.

TV advertisers can say, "You are a unique individual, with special gifts and talents," yet at the same time try to sell you something based on the idea that you are not going to be accepted unless you are young, beautiful, slim, or have a well-sculpted body. Some of us are told we are the "wrong" color; some are the "wrong" height, or we just don't wear the "right" clothes. Can you even imagine how boring the world would be if we all came out of the same mold—same color, same hair, same personality, nothing to distinguish us from the person next door? Yet many of us are afraid of the unknown and find security in trying to be like everyone else. We have the ability to embrace the sheer beauty of uniqueness and individuality, but instead we often spend inordinate amounts of time and energy working to look like everyone around us!

The key to understanding yourself and your own journey of separation is in recognizing that many of us share these fears of the unknown, of becoming our own separate and responsible person, and of owning our own choices. Your alternative to pursuing separation is to continue following the trends, whether or not you agree with them. You are free to stay within the realm of what you have already experienced, remaining fearful that if you did explore some new area of the world, the whole framework of your life would be in jeopardy. We can also fear the unknown areas of our own psyche. These fears, however, keep us from the growth and change necessary to become whole. We keep ourselves from the love and wholeness we want.

As you face the fears of your own distinctness and discover your own separateness and individuality, it is important that you do not aggressively push yourself out into the world of adulthood or stuff your fears down inside. You now have the opportunity to awaken your longings to choose, to be separate, to direct yourself, to grow into adulthood, and to freely *let go* of your reluctance to become yourself.

Let's move on to discover how remaining enmeshed and unseparated causes us to be constantly waiting and relying on others to provide happiness for us.

## The Waiting Game

We explore with our clients the reasons they are invested in remaining in a passive, confused position instead of determining their direction and taking hold of happiness. We ask, "What are you waiting for?" The clients, time after time, look at us bewildered: "I am not waiting for anything! What are you talking about?" Many of us do not even realize we have been putting our lives on hold for years!

We can relate—feeling stuck, frustrated, impatient, or busy, with few results. Let's look to the secret of the ways many of us place ourselves in a waiting position. Once we see patterns, of which we have been unaware, we can empower and free ourselves.

What we both have discovered is that we all engage in disguised and hidden forms of waiting. None of us really wants to admit, "Yeah! I always put my life on hold and, even though I am forty, I am still waiting for my parents to come and take care of me." Instead of acknowledging this, we make our defenses more palatable. We push our actions into places in our psyche that we cannot see. We often hide these secret forms of waiting from our own conscious mind because we are used to the "waiting and wanting" role.

For example, instead of admitting to yourself, *I am afraid of intimacy,* you ask yourself, *I wonder why everyone I keep choosing to date runs from intimacy? If only these other people would turn around and join me here in this intimate relationship, everything would be fine!* You do not even consider the notion that *perhaps* you are afraid of intimacy or you would not keep choosing distant people to try to connect with.

Once we recognize that we are putting ourselves in the powerless, passive position of a victim, we can begin to access our power to choose and move into an active position, directing ourselves where we want to go.

Moving out of a "victim" position requires conscious effort. This is especially the case if in our childhood we were victims of abuse, neglect, or rejection. We were powerless as children and relied on adults to protect us. If an adult was not protecting us, we did as much as we could as children, but mostly we waited and hoped for some kind adult to see the abuse and intervene.

When we met a kind adult, we may have desperately wanted to ask for help, yet we were ashamed to reveal the wounds that had been inflicted on us. If this part within us was just buried, glazed over, and/or "forgotten," then, most likely it has developed into something extremely toxic. Perhaps our hunger for love has now become insatiable. We move to a place where we give up almost anything to keep someone else around. Others of us feel so bad about ourselves now that we think we do not deserve anything more than an abusive relationship.

We will look now at three specific ways we subconsciously choose to put our lives on hold, keeping ourselves in a passive childlike position. As we discover what these ways are, we will give ourselves the opportunity to actively assert ourselves and determine our direction as adults.

1. When we are running around trying to be perfect or successful to gain outward approval, we are *waiting for someone else to make us worthy.*
2. When we are holding on to anger and resentment, unwilling to forgive and let go, we are *waiting for someone's apology or for vengeance on him or her.*
3. When we are looking for people just like our parents, investing inordinate amounts of time trying to fix them, thinking somehow they will fill up the holes in our soul created by our parents, we are *waiting for reciprocity.*

My clients are surprised when they recognize themselves in at least one of the above secret ways of remaining passive. We continue each of these forms of waiting because we *think* we will become more powerful in our waiting position. We think we are offering ourselves more protection in the long run, but the results will show that we take away from our own wholeness and growth. Whenever we offer ourselves the "easy way out," we risk making ourselves weaker by continually taking it.

### Waiting for Someone Else to Make Us Worthy

The first pattern of hidden waiting is that of waiting for someone else to define our worth or make us feel valuable. We do not think we are *waiting* because we are literally *moving* all the time. We become so busy running around eliciting the approval of others that we forget we are still in a waiting position, waiting for another person to define our worth. Instead of learning what it is to be comfortable in our own skin and appreciate where we are, we search for others to tell us we are lovable. We have the ability to spend our time and energy defining and creating ourselves, encouraging ourselves toward where we *wish* to go. Instead, we give our time and energy away.

When we run around searching for and trying to live up to everyone else's expectations, agendas, or standards of acceptance, we place ourselves in a continuous repetition of childhood. We do not realize we are separate, adult, human beings who have the ability to be our own person. We spend our time trying to make enough money, wear the right clothes, have the perfect number of children, buy the car with the most features, or live in an acceptable area. We are still secretly trying to live up to our parents' ideals, to live within their "boxes"—but we do not want to think that our parents are controlling us, so we replace them with the everyday trends that surround us. We try to "keep up with the Joneses." They are our authorities now. They are our parents. They define our worth and direct us in how we invest our time and energy as adults.

What happens to discovering what we like to wear, where we wish to live, what kind of family we desire to create and nurture, what values and standards we wish to live out in our daily lives? To discover and let go of this kind of passivity is to grow up, to become a separate adult, and to explore new territory. We have the ability within us to succeed apart from our parents, to discover our individuality. The process begins by refusing to find our worth in what everyday society considers valuable—and by walking toward God as we understand him and ourselves as we are beginning to understand ourselves—and by learning what it is to have worth outside of financial worth or productivity worth. It is time to discover our internal worth, inherent in us as God's creation.

### Waiting for Someone's Apology or for Vengeance

There are many books on forgiveness. Here we can only briefly explore what forgiveness looks like and summarize the primary ways this hidden pattern of passive waiting for apologies is destructive.

Waiting for an apology is a very subtle form of passivity. We hardly realize we are doing it. We often think it is the best self-protection when we hold on to our anger and resentment toward someone who has harmed us.

Anger, we will learn, is an indicator that we do not feel protected, that some boundary of ours has been violated, neglected, or disregarded. When we explore the physiological reactions we are causing when we hold on to anger, we will see exactly what "waiting for an apology" does to us.

Our brains run on a chemical called serotonin. When we have enough serotonin in our brains, we feel happy, sleep well, are at peace, and function well in life. When our serotonin is depleted, we feel tired and irritable and can't concentrate. We wake up in the middle of the night and have difficulty falling back asleep. Whenever we hold on to grudges, anger, and resentment, we are depleting the serotonin in our brains.

Thus we see that when we wait for another to come to us and apologize for some destructive behavior, we are causing our own physiological damage. We depress ourselves as we expend our energy waiting for the apology and holding tightly to our bitterness, pain, resentment, and anger.

Five to 10 percent of us inherit a below-average ability to produce serotonin and have tendencies to experience prolonged depression unless we are able to boost serotonin production with medication. For this small percentage, normalizing medications can be a lifelong process that brings lifelong benefits.

Our mind/body combination is a complex structure that is affected not only by genetic predispositions (for some) but also by nutrition, the nurturing we received in childhood, our present resentment and anger, and many other factors. We have the ability to aggravate whatever is more vulnerable or susceptible within us. The angrier we remain the more vulnerable we are to strokes, heart attacks, and most other diseases.

Most of us inherit an adequate serotonin level but deplete it by holding on to anger or resentment toward others and ourselves. This happens when we are unwilling to forgive others and unwilling to forgive ourselves for past failures. This choice leads us to a place where we become more depressed and less functional. When we lower our serotonin level, we also lower our resistance to physical diseases, which may actually lead to death. I (Paul) learned in medical school that repressed anger is the leading cause of death. As we start to forgive and let go of our anger we slowly restore our serotonin to normal levels.

The alternative to waiting for an apology is *forgiveness*. This does not mean that we invite the person to continue being destructive to us. This means, instead, that we are no longer going to let our lives be controlled by how mad he or she makes us (that is often exactly what the person wants!). We can choose to recognize the hurtful behavior, recognize the act as unjust, then seek God for wisdom on how to offer love to that person (while still protecting ourselves from inviting the same thing to happen again). We see a common value in religions that express, "Love your neighbor as yourself." We know this does not mean to indulge yourself by giving yourself tons of excuses, letting yourself off the hook, and planning to do the same destructive thing again. This means to offer yourself love. In the same way, we do not indulge the person who is destructive toward us, but we offer him or her our love.

The process of forgiveness is hard for most of us. To understand a Jewish perspective on forgiveness, we can look to the Torah and explore the ways sins were atoned for. Not one drop of blood was shed without God accounting for it. Here is a commentary by Rabbi Nosson Scherman on atonement for sin as described in the Book of Leviticus.

> The Torah now lists offerings that are required in order to atone for sins . . . (Leviticus 4).
>
> These offerings cannot atone for sins that were committed intentionally. No offering is sufficient to remove the stain of such sinfulness; that can be done only through repentance and a change of the attitude that made it possible for the transgressor to flout God's will. . . . Sin offerings are needed to atone for deeds that were committed בִּשְׁגָגָ, inadvertently, as a result of carelessness. . . . Even though they were unintentional, such deeds blemish the soul and require that it be purified, for if the sinner had sincerely regarded them with the proper gravity, the violations would not have occurred. As experience teaches, peo-

71

ple are careful about things that matter to them, but tend to be careless about trivialities.

This provides perspective on the Torah's view of sin. It provides no "ritual" to atone for intentional sins; only God can see into a man's heart and judge whether he has truly repented.[4]

We read in both the Old and New Testaments: "Vengeance is mine, saith the Lord." God will account for all wrong. He does not want us to take vengeance into our own hands but assures us that he will make all wrongs right. In other words, all wrongs will be repaid.

Some of us think, *I can let my anger go in this circumstance,* because we know that the person committing the destructive act will bring destruction back on himself. There is a Proverb that reads, "He who digs a pit will himself fall into it."

The Christian perspective reveals that the destruction the person committed will be accounted for. No one gets away with his destructive behavior: "Do not be deceived: God cannot be mocked. A man reaps what he sows" (Gal. 6:7 NIV). Jesus, being perfect, died to atone for each person's act(s) of separation and brokenness from God. We can choose to refuse this provision for restored intimacy and continue to walk in a place of disharmony with God and ourselves, or we can choose to be reconciled to one another and to God through Jesus.

When we look at the word *atone,* we see the words *at* and *one.* To atone is to bring that which is imperfect and separated from God back to a place of oneness, wholeness, holy again before a holy God. God's standard of perfection is much greater than any of ours, yet his love is also much greater. We know in ancient Israel, when a woman was caught committing adultery, the law required her to be stoned. Yet when such a woman was brought to Jesus, he stood before her accusers and said, "He who is without sin among you, let him throw a stone at her first" (John 8:7), and then he began writing on the ground. As he did, the accusers walked away one by one. Then Jesus looked at the woman and asked, " 'Woman, where are those accusers of yours? Has no one condemned you?' She said, 'No one, Lord.'

And Jesus said to her, 'Neither do I condemn you; go and sin no more'" (vv. 10–11).

The profound teachings of Jesus remind us:

> Judge not, and you shall not be judged. Condemn not, and you shall not be condemned. Forgive, and you will be forgiven. Give, and it will be given to you. . . . For with the same measure that you use, it will be measured back to you.
>
> Luke 6:37–38

In this we are again reminded of the importance of forgiveness. We can learn what it is to extend love to a person and forgive—while still choosing to protect ourselves from his or her hurtfulness. For instance: I can agree that the man who sold me my car deceitfully ripped me off, yet I can choose to let go of my bitterness and anger toward him (each time it occurs within me) and extend love. There is no way that I would return to the same car dealership or buy anything else from this man, yet I know that ultimately he stands before God with what he has sown, and God has provided a way to reconcile this man to himself, if the man will let go of and turn from his deceit and accept God's provision. I know also, if I live with hatred and anger burning within me, I become as broken and twisted as those whom I hate. Is one "jerk" really worth my going through months of depression? I don't think so. So I forgive (give love before he deserves it) and turn vengeance over to God.

### Waiting for Reciprocity

If a girl grows up with an alcoholic father, the odds are that when it is time for her to marry, she will choose an alcoholic—because it is familiar, or so that she can subconsciously feel like she is fixing her father. If her husband gets help, quits being an alcoholic, and begins to live an independent life, connected to others and wanting to connect with her, she will, in many cases, divorce him and marry another alcoholic whom she can unconsciously enable and reward while she consciously thinks she is

73

trying to fix him. In our practices we see this pattern over and over again.

I (Paul) love Tina Turner's song "What's Love Got to Do with It?" because in her song she recognizes that what we call love is just a "secondhand emotion" that we transfer from a parent to a parental substitute. This is why, when a boy grows up with a controlling mother, he will most often "fall in love" with women who will control him. What does love really have to do with his choice? He wants to fix his mother or be in the same kind of controlling environment. In doing this, he passively and unconsciously stays in the rut that he has become accustomed to.

Waiting for reciprocity means spending countless hours, days, months, and years waiting for a distant and disconnected other to change and meet our unmet needs from childhood. We could be using all this time to learn how to and begin to meet our own needs and provide for ourselves—connecting with ourselves and friends who *do* love and accept us for the way we are. But instead, we waste our lives blaming and waiting for someone who is incapable of, or unwilling to, relate intimately. It is important that we teach ourselves to let them go. God said in Psalm 68 that he loves those of us who are lonely and desires to place us in new, healthier "families."

If you are already married to someone who is disconnected, you can let go of waiting for him or her to come and fill your needs. You do not have to divorce your partner to develop an intimate knowledge of yourself. Nor do you need your spouse's permission to form an intimate relationship with God and friends. Of course, when a marriage is strained, it often results in a lack of physical intimacy. Though we were created to enjoy this kind of intimacy in our marriages, we will not die without it. Sexual intimacy is beautiful and wonderful, yet there are other viable forms of intimacy one can learn to enjoy.

We can wait in bitterness and loneliness or let go of waiting and learn how to direct our own path to true meaning, purpose, and happiness. We can read, share, learn from others, and figure out how to be fulfilled—instead of waiting for one person to come along to whom we assign magical powers. (This is what happens to people who fall into religious and secular cults or political groups with one magical and dominant leader.)

Our secret waiting patterns are so disguised we are hardly aware, until something happens to make us aware, that we really are waiting. Remember, as long as we are in a waiting position

- our lives are on hold
- our hope is outside of ourselves
- we are helpless to change because we sit and wait (like a child waits for Mommy to feed him or her)

This is our opportunity to choose to be gentle with ourselves, especially concerning our past mistakes, and yet have the courage to change. It is wonderful to choose not to be judgmental but to ask, *What am I offering myself?* and *Why am I not offering myself the best that God has to offer?* Often we stay in a horrible situation because we have never brought ourselves to a safe enough place (even in our imaginations) where we have new options. It is important for us to finally see the truth that the options we have been holding on to so tightly are not the only solutions available to us anymore.

This is not to be confused with the virtue of patience. I have seen so many people get mad at themselves for not being "patient" enough: "Henry is out drinking again. This is the fourth night this week he decided to go to happy hour with his friends from work instead of picking the kids up from school. I'm glad he still goes to work every day. I need to just be patient with him and hope that God will change his heart." (Henry may even say, "Just be patient with me, Martha!")

Yes, you want God to change Henry's heart, but his actions are destructive *right now* to himself, the marriage, the kids, the whole family. When you tell yourself that you need more patience, you are accepting the blame for Henry's behavior and placing yourself and your kids in the powerless position of waiting. When you do this to yourself, you begin to feel weaker and weaker inside, because in following this action you are behaving as if you are powerless to take care of yourself. You become what you train yourself to become. And Henry probably won't change unless you set up boundaries to protect yourself and the kids from his alcoholism.

Alcoholics usually don't change until they hit rock bottom. By standing up to Henry, you are actually loving and helping him more than your previous behavior, which enabled him. You cannot make him change, but you can choose not to subject yourself and your children to the dangers of alcoholism. God won't make your mate change against his own wishes. When your mate asks for God to intervene, God will surely be there.

We can be patient when we are waiting for our baby to be born. We can be patient when we are waiting for a stoplight to turn green. We can be patient with the mother who is walking her two children across the street. But it is preposterous to be patient while waiting for a brick wall to turn into a door. We can spend our whole life waiting for that to happen, or we can decide to take control of our own life, doing the things that will bring us fulfillment and joy.

## Becoming an Active Adult

Adults are called to courageously let go of childlike confusion and waiting. Our needs are no longer needs that we will die from when they are not met by others. We have the ability to provide for our wants and discover what we like. It is now no longer anyone else's fault that our lives are on hold. If we want to unstick ourselves from whomever or whatever we have stuck ourselves to, it is time to unstick—and in so doing open the opportunity for genuine connection with others! It is precisely when we are adults, separate, making our own choices and taking responsibility for our choices, that we discover the amazing joy of forming intimate friendships with others. In becoming our own person and owning our own choices, we initiate clarity instead of confusion. We move to a place of real and honest self-awareness. In this process we become awakened to many of the places within ourselves that are not yet full of love and truth. This honest look does not mean we look at ourselves with the critical eye of our disapproving parent or with the eyes of self-condemnation. This process of ownership of self and self's actions is one in which we are becoming whole. We are growing in maturity from the dependence of infancy, the transition of childhood, to the separation and the formation of intimate relationships of adulthood. We are on a quest for wholeness, and wholeness, we discover, is "healthy, unhurt, entire, recovered from a wound or injury: *restored,* healed, complete, unbroken, perfect." When we look up the word *holy,* we read, "akin to Old English *hal:* whole."

We carry within us a recollection that we were made in the image of a holy God. We recognize that we have the ability to think abstractly, to reason, to direct ourselves toward that which we know in our hearts is good, true, or beautiful. We also have the ability to neglect or abuse this gift of choice. We are not governed merely by instinct, but we have access to endless possibilities of action.

When Mother Teresa was questioned about her calling in life she immediately responded with an answer she had already contemplated and known well within her heart:

> *Each one* of us is what he is in the eyes of God. We are all called to be saints. Holiness isn't a luxury reserved for only a few but a simple duty for all of us. There is nothing extraordinary about this call. We all have been created in the image of God to love and be loved.[5]

Mother Teresa knew well her personal calling in life. Many of us look at someone as kind as Mother Teresa was and think, *I am very far from being a saint.* The word *holy,* as we discovered, means "set apart, consecrated," consecrated for a particular purpose. When we choose to create holy lives, we are saying in essence that our lives are purposeful. We agree with God that there is a particular purpose we were sent here to discover and fulfill. We each have the choice to see if this is something we want for ourselves. If we do not enjoy our lives more and have richer, fuller lives from making choices, we can always go back to letting others decide for us.

When we invite wisdom to teach us how to develop wholeness in our emotions, spirit, mind, and body, we begin each day with our end goal in mind, with an idea of the person we would like to become. Now is your opportunity to step out of ambivalence and into making choices, determining your direction, recognizing your deeper purposes, and creating a more meaningful life for yourself. In doing so, you will direct yourself toward a full life that you are attracted to and will enjoy. It is in this process of seeking wisdom to purposefully direct your path that you reclaim yourself, re-member yourself back to a place of wholeness, and learn what it is to take yourself out of a *victim* position and out of a *waiting* position and place yourself into a *powerful and whole (holy) life.*

# Part 2

# DETECTION

We detect and define the areas in our lives that we wish to change, that are still unhealed. We ask ourselves: What fears am I prepared to let go to give myself the love and healing I want?

# five

# Cave Sweet Cave

A prisoner who is condemned to solitude . . . will in the long run, especially if the run is too long, suffer from the effects as surely as one who has gone hungry for too long. Like everyone else, I need friendly or affectionate relationships or intimate companionship, and am not made of stone . . . and like any man of culture or decency I cannot do without these things and not feel a void, a lack of something—and I tell you all this to let you know how much good your visit has done me.

Vincent van Gogh

You are fortunate; you are not a prisoner condemned to solitude. You may at times feel like you are a prisoner of your circumstances, yet now you are pursuing your ability to take a more direct and active role in recognizing and consciously changing the choices you make for your own life.

In this chapter we will explore some of the reasons why we retreat to our caves or think by running away we are providing ourselves with the best solution to our problems. We will also move toward understanding the "cave dwellers" in our lives and learn how to stop spending all our energy trying to drag them out. Remember, you have the freedom to love and be loved. No one but you can stop you from being kind to yourself or accessing the love of God.

You are learning what it means to carry this out. If you long for affection and intimate companionship, it is important that you acquire the skills and tools necessary to create an environment in which you can enjoy those things. Even though you may have the tendency to live in isolation for long periods at a time, you do not have to continue like this forever. Your life is yours. You were not created for isolation, yet you have the freedom to give yourself isolation. Take a moment for an exercise that will help you understand yourself and assess where you are on your path toward love. In this exercise you will give answers that may surprise you. You will usually give yourself the best results if you write down the first answers that come to mind.

## Cave Dweller Exercise

1. If I could have made two requests of my mom while growing up and she was magically able to grant me these requests, I would have wanted my mom to:

   a. be more _____ and _____

   b. be less _____ and _____

2. If I could have made two requests of my dad while growing up and he was magically able to grant me these requests, I would have wanted my dad to:

   a. be more _____ and _____

   b. be less _____ and _____

3. Am I giving myself the most meaningful and enjoyable existence that I can create? Yes/No

If yes, write out three ways you have created this for your-self:

_____

_____

_____

If no, name three things that you would like to change about your life:

_____

_____

_____

4. Look at your answers above and ask yourself: What am I desiring from these changes? For example, if you answered, "I'd like to be less angry," your desire is to feel safe, loved, and unthreatened. If you answered, "I'd like to get along better with people at work," your desire is peace, to be liked by others, and for others to enjoy your company and you to enjoy theirs. If you answered, "Fight less with my spouse," you desire closeness, love, and connection. Now describe what you desire:

I desire _____

I desire _____

I desire _____

5. I have not made the changes that I listed in question 3 and have not given myself what I truly desire because (try not to attribute the cause to someone else, like your spouse or boss):

_____

_____

_____

6. Now, fill in the blanks with your answers from questions 1 and 2 to see how well they fit:

I create a more meaningful and enjoyable life for myself when I am more (1a) _____, _____, (2a) _____, and _____ to myself.
I sometimes sabotage my own happiness by being (1b) _____, _____, (2b) _____, and _____ to myself.

## Waiting for Spring

At times it may seem like all of your energy is spent either running to your cave or trying to drag someone else out of theirs! Either way you feel the pain of isolation. Your life was made for more love than this.

You may be deep within your cave, hibernating through winter, waiting for spring. What you may not realize is that *this* spring does not arrive three months after the onset of winter; rather it begins when you wake up. For it is your heart that may be hibernating, and only when you choose to rouse it and experience life and the love around you will spring arrive.

As it turns out, we all have cave-dwelling tendencies, tendencies to isolate and pull away from others. Some part of us does not think the words "happily ever after" apply to us. We still long for happiness, so we create a cave and try to find our happiness alone. As much as we want to be loved, the idea of relating to others is somewhat frightening. We fear that we will be rejected or criticized, so we stay secluded and feel "safe" for the moment.

Safety is important. The problem is, when we are not in loving relationships with others, our hearts grow cold. Our hearts were formed to be in relationship. Just as it takes two sticks rubbed together to create a fire, so also the warmth that we can create from loving and being loved is the warmth that causes our hearts to be nurtured. When our hearts are loved, we feel safe to grow and become all that we were meant to become.

Of course, if we were constantly rejected as a child, we do not know very much warmth, so we think the safety of a cave will provide us with everything we need. We think that at least it will provide more than what is "out there," outside of the cave.

When we do not feel at home in relationships, we each scatter to our own caves. The phrase "home sweet home" does not apply to our relationships. Our minds imprison our hearts by creating the only solution we think will work: "cave sweet cave." Eventually, though, we find that the cave is much colder than it is sweet, and we miss the warmth of friendship.

There is a beautiful passage written by the prophet Ezekiel. He is speaking the words of God to Israel: "I will give you a new heart and put a new spirit in you; I will remove from you your heart of stone and give you a heart of flesh. . . . You will be my people, and I will be your God" (36:26, 28 NIV). How unlike that of unloving or rejecting parents is the provision of God! The passage continues, "I will call for the grain and make it plentiful and will not bring famine upon you" (v. 29).

It is clearly not God's intention that we remain spiritually empty, with hearts as cold as stone. We were made to be in relationship, so why do we dwell in caves?

> We do not feel worthy enough to come out of our cave.
> We feel safer inside.
> We do not wish to be rejected or criticized.
> We do not want others to demand things from us.
> We don't trust relationships in general.

We can begin to understand the psychological dynamics within us that influence our desire to escape into our personal caves. Here is a story about Peter, who often withdrew to his cave.

## Peter's Story

Peter grew up in an environment where both of his parents were consistently critical of him. His father was usually either at work or in the living room drinking a glass of brandy. His mother (Jane) was usually away from home, involved in all sorts of societies and functions. When she was home, she held a "special" place in her heart for Peter. Her relationship with her husband had long since dissolved. As much as Jane had tried, her husband would not respond to her. So Jane often looked for affection from her only child, Peter.

Peter, who felt alienated from his distant father, had a keen understanding and sensitivity to his mother's feelings of being forsaken and disconnected. For years he would long for his father to join him in playing with model trains or take him fishing on the lake or teach him how to ride his bike. His father always said that he was too busy or needed to relax, so Peter stopped hoping. Peter created his own imaginative world inside and built a wall around himself.

Though he often desired to retreat to his cave, from time to time Peter felt compelled to come out and do the best he could to care for his mom and make up for his father's lack of attention. He felt sorry for his mother, so he accepted her plea for love as his responsibility.

Peter was haunted by the fear that dating a woman would somehow betray his mother. Peter had already accepted the responsibility to make up for what his dad failed to do. Part of Peter wondered, *Who is going to take care of Mom's need to be loved if I betray her like my father has?*

In dating relationships Peter also struggled with trying to live up to the male role model he had learned from his father. From him he learned that a man does not draw near to women. A man treats women with disrespect. Whenever Peter felt inclined to pursue a relationship with a woman, he felt inadequate as a man. He had some idea, buried deep inside, that if he became the pursuer in the relationship, he would feel extremely needy. He would often begin to express interest in a particular woman, then immediately become aloof and retreat to his cave, ashamed of the perceived neediness he despised.

Due to his self-punitive nature, which he learned from his critical parents, he put himself down and felt angry at himself for having romantic feelings for women his age. As soon as he stepped out enough to get to know a woman, his mom would criticize his efforts so that he wouldn't continue. His mother struggled to keep the manufactured love and affection she was used to receiving from her *little* boy. In no way did she want a young woman to come and steal her little boy's heart away. She thought there would be no love left over for her.

Peter soon began to feel the burden of trying to fulfill his mother's need for attention. After he progressed through the awkward stages of adolescence, he began to date women who were surprisingly similar to his parents. His girlfriends would either crave endless amounts of attention from him or would be cold, disinterested, and unattached. Whenever one of his girlfriends expressed anything resembling an expectation, he felt suffocated, just like he felt when his mother wouldn't leave him alone. He found that the only way to retreat was to move into his psychological cave and tell them, "I'm too busy," or "I need some time to relax."

He thought, in retreating to his cave, that he was exerting his strength, protecting himself, and providing for himself. His retreat was rewarded by the fact that he was removed from his mother's demands and the demands he perceived his girl-friends were making. By acting on his fear and retreating to his cave, he took away opportunity after opportunity to learn how to set boundaries within himself and with others. He was making himself weaker while disabling the growth of his social and emotional skills. He didn't give himself the opportunity to learn what it was to say no, to really look at and discover what his responsibilities truly were and where his responsibilities ended. By taking away the opportunities for the growth that he needed, Peter was creating a crisis in his life. By acting con-sistently on his fear and his wish to avoid problems, he taught himself how to be even more insecure about coming out of his cave.

Instead of embracing the wonders of committing to himself and engaging in intimate relationships, he made choices to retreat or to keep busy with numerous superficial relationships that allowed him to keep one foot in his cave. Peter used these acquaintances to meet, on a superficial level, his longing for connection. He avoided more intimate relationships that required so much more of his presence. This scared him because he felt insecure about his innermost self. Somewhere inside he thought, *If my own father didn't have the time of day for me, then why would anyone else really wish to know who I truly am?* He felt that to be present with others, he would be expected to come out of his cave, where he felt vulnerable and exposed. By keeping himself in his cave, he thought he was protecting himself. He eventually learned, however, that when he made his cave his home, he withdrew his opportunity to love and to be truly loved.

## Dealing with Half-Truths

When you were a child, there may have been no safe place for you to come out and feel comfortable with yourself and to say *no* without guilt. Now, as an adult, you can choose to create such a place. It is important for you to feel comfortable with saying *no* and *yes*. When you give yourself this freedom, your *yes* becomes meaningful. Your *no* truly sets a limit. All of us, to some extent, have an idea in our mind that the distance we keep between ourselves and others will safeguard us from pain. This is true in part, yet such half-truths are often the most deceptive and destroy our inner growth. Wherever we discover a half-truth, we must search for the real truth it is covering up.

### *Responsibility*

Let's consider the meaning of *responsibility*. It is the ability to respond to self and others. When you run away from responsibility because you are overwhelmed or full of fear, you also run away from your ability to engage in relationships with others. You run away from your *ability*. You limit yourself. You create a disabled self. When you take away your power in this way, you increasingly feel like you have to run and hide from those you perceive as demanding. You open the door to fear, which can overwhelm you. You become so afraid of being criticized that you do not engage and access the creative parts of yourself that long to awaken within you.

As a child what else can you do? Where else can you go? You escape in your closet, in your imagination, in a book, wherever you can go to keep the invaders out. You are small and innocent, with little power to protect you from danger. As an adult, however, you have the opportunity to do something. You can encourage yourself to face your fears.

A child is limited in his or her ability to protect self. An adult, however, is faced with a world of choices that were not available in childhood. If a person does not consciously choose to open his or her eyes to the new possibilities, they will remain buried, hidden deep in the back of the cave.

### Fear

Sadly, Peter thought that fear and hiding were his only answers. He thought that to make up for his father's lack of caring, he would care for himself by retreating to his cave. In his cave he discovered he was not loving himself but tearing himself apart with this fear and anger. He pushed down on his own feelings, shutting them up in the coldness of the cave, and thus he became depressed.

By now you have discovered many of the ways you can block these choices from your conscious awareness. Your childhood fear can still live within you, especially if you choose to feed it with more fear. In doing so you enable the fear to block your choices. The problem is, as with any buried pain, like an undiscovered cancer it grows and begins to permeate other parts of the psyche. Depression and held-in anger cause physiological changes, which can lead to death. Van Gogh was not altogether wrong in his intuitive understanding that "a prisoner who is condemned to solitude . . . will in the long run, especially if the run is too long, suffer from the effects as surely as one who has gone hungry for too long."

As adults we have the ability to feed ourselves. We have the ability, if we use it, to learn how to develop and form unbreakable bonds, intimate connections with others who are safe. When we become safe with ourselves, treating ourselves with respect and affection, we find we become comfortable sharing ourselves with others. We are no longer prisoners, condemned to our cave, as we may have been in childhood. As adults we are "just as big" as our parents, we are able to release ourselves from our caves, and we can find other ways to protect ourselves from those who wish to harm us.

### *The Power of Love*

When you invest in that which is beyond your fear—love, the place where courage, self-awareness, and self-discipline can take you—you have a deeper connection with yourself and with life, and you find you can engage more intimately with others. You run to the cave less often, because you hold within yourself an inner strength that you have learned to develop by not retreating to the cave. You, Peter, or any other adult cave dweller can make the choice to create "home sweet home" where love reigns in warmth instead of "cave sweet cave" where fear reigns in coldness. To do this it is important that you encourage (infuse courage in) yourself. You let go of fear and give yourself the opportunity to develop your love ability.

*Love ability* is the ability to

- respond to yourself
- take care of yourself
- say no, refusing to take on everyone else's responsibilities and expectations
- teach yourself that your own self-expectations are at times inordinate (overwhelming) and thus keep you inoperative (emotionally disabled)
- let go of your self-criticism and learn to adopt more loving, gentle ways of connecting with yourself and others
- discover and create your true self
- initiate your selfhood and identity

## A Note for the Cave Dweller's Significant Other

If you feel like you are constantly dragging someone out of his or her cave or finding one cave dweller after another, or if you have been married to a cave dweller for quite some time now, we have important information for you.

- You deserve more love than a cave dweller gives you.
- You deserve more love than you are currently giving yourself.

This does *not* mean, if you are married to a spouse-in-a-cave, that you ought to divorce this person. God gave us marriage as a gift. You chose the person you are with for a reason. When you stay and do not run from your opportunity to form your own boundaries and limits, you give yourself the chance to grow and heal. If you leave your spouse today without giving yourself the opportunity for self-awareness and growth, you will almost certainly choose another cave dweller as a partner.

Just because we leave a broken relationship does not mean we leave our brokenness behind. How much beauty we could invite back into this world if we would choose to stay in our marriage, love our broken spouse and our broken self, and heal our deep wounds! It breaks my heart that we do not recognize the love in God's voice, tenderly encouraging us to stay and learn how to heal within the bonds of our commitment.

You deserve more love than a cave dweller gives you. Learn how to invite that love into your life. Learn how to increase your own love ability. Recognize the reality that the cave dweller in your life deserves more love than he or she gives to him- or herself. He or she can remain broken. You can grieve that brokenness. You can begin to heal your own brokenness by embracing the love that has been available to you your whole life from God, real friends, and yourself. Take back your energy that you keep giving away by trying to drag the cave dweller out of the cave. Let go, or you create your own cave. Embrace love. Invite your partner to join you, but allow him or her the freedom to choose. Protect yourself and embrace love, even though it is difficult to do.

## Common Pitfalls

Here are four pitfalls that are common when people first learn to come out of the cave.

### *Pride in Our Defenses*

Many of us are proud of our defenses, especially if we did not have a father who was proud of our accomplishments and who we were. We become proud that we have learned to protect ourselves from the pain we have felt from abandonment and/or distance. For so long we have worked to block out rejection that it is difficult to take down the blockades and let love in, but part of love is being humble and receptive enough to accept it. The whole world is not like the critical, neglectful, or distant people who raised us or to whom we are married. Love is waiting to live within each of us. We can welcome this love like a child again, yet this time without fear, because we are big enough to protect ourselves now.

We wonder at Jesus' rebuke to his disciples who did not understand the mystery of childlikeness, "Let the little children come to me, and do not hinder them, for the kingdom of God belongs to such as these. I tell you the truth, anyone who will not receive the kingdom of God like a little child will never enter it" (Luke 18:16–17 NIV). And he held the children and blessed them. Children warmly accept affection and love; they are innocent and carefree. We as adults can invite this kind of childlike excitement and wonder to be alive in us as we mature into responsive and engaging adults.

### *Fear of the Unknown*

Now that we have the possibility for real intimacy, many of us find we run from it. Our parents did not model intimacy, so it is unfamiliar. We are somewhat suspicious and scared of it.

We were all probably afraid to walk or ride our bikes for the first time because it was new and awkward, yet once we experienced our own mobility, we dreamed of learning to fly! It can be the same with love and intimacy. Be gentle with yourself. If you learn what it is to listen to and attend to yourself, you build up an inner trust, believing that you are able to protect yourself and trust yourself with others. You are not like Peter's mom, waiting for others to fill you up. You are on an active adventure of truly learning what it is to be connected with your thoughts, feelings, likes, and dislikes, to be connected with God, with nature, and with people around you.

### Putting Up Walls

Beware, and be aware, of your old ways of constant criticism, anger toward self (unforgiveness), and biting sarcasm. These three are all walls that we erect without even realizing it, yet we feel the painful result of their presence. We are like a turtle wanting to come out of his shell and hang out with the other turtles around him. His self-criticism and sarcasm, however, make him feel more and more insecure, so he feels like he must either fight to prove himself or retreat deeper into his shell.

We become angry and critical or sarcastic because we feel vulnerable and unprotected. Instead of criticizing, try to discover where you are hurting and choose to use your energy caring for and protecting that part of yourself with love. Forgive yourself. Imagine what it is to be gentle, protective, forgiving.

### The Allure of Aloofness

Let go of the idea that the one in the relationship who is the most aloof and distant is the most powerful. This, again, is a half-truth that enslaves us when we believe it. Erroneously, we think that there are only two kinds of people in relationships—the needy person and the aloof person. Because of the malnourishment in our past, many of us have developed inordinate needs for love, which we try desperately to push down. We

93

try to act aloof. In our aloofness we try to make ourselves indispensable to others, to the people we want to connect with, so that they need us instead of our needing them. We find other needy people to need us, then we soon resent their neediness because it reminds us of our own secret inner neediness, which we detest.

We do not realize that there is an option that we haven't seen. We have the option of connecting with the "needy" part of ourself. We can choose to love that part of ourself to health. When we connect with this lonely part of ourself, we discover that we no longer have to be afraid of our own inner longings for love and connectedness. We do not have to be afraid of others' longings for connection either. Being aloof to our own longings or to theirs did not result in bringing us what we wanted. It only created more pain. Connect with yourself and your longings; discover all of the beautiful ways love wishes to engage with you!

There are beautiful places of belonging that your soul has been aching to experience, so go to these places, Encourage yourself to join some kind of small group, whether the group is centered around a hobby or a study of a particular subject. You will see that others start out feeling just as awkward or more so than you. We learn to love by loving. Visit a lonely person—a foster child, an elderly person, or someone in jail or a hospital. Join them in their loneliness so that they too can have warmth. You can bring it to them. Let go of the cave and experience the love you were intended to enjoy!

If you think of belonging as longing to be yourself as you truly are, this helps you to find specific places you can feel this kind of unconditional acceptance. This is difficult, perhaps the most difficult thing our patients face when they come to Dallas for the day program. They sit in group therapy for three hours a day with a therapist and an additional three hours a day of group educational therapy. Most of our patients are resistant to working in this kind of group setting at first, but it ends up being the most effective way to get to the healing. You see and experience others who are willing to accept you just as you are. You no longer have to hide your pain or secrets or hide behind a mask. As the others warm up to the real you, you warm up to yourself.

## Wrapping Up

You have begun to discover some of your defenses that worked well to protect you as a child. Now you have the opportunity to develop new adult forms of protection and let go of insisting that the cave is the only way.

It is important to remember that both men and women can create their own form of cave. Sometimes the cave is more subtle and much more difficult to detect than Peter's, for example, depression, anxiety, eating disorders, workaholism, churchaholism. Alcoholism, drug addiction, or any form of addiction can become a cave. If you are still choosing to stay in a cave, wishing someone would care enough to rescue you and save you from yourself, know that love is available right now. You deserve more fullness than any addiction offers. You deserve love and not the fear that binds you. No one can force you out of the cave. You may resent your loved ones for trying or for not trying hard enough. You have the ability to embrace love and walk away from the cave. This process of coming out is not about forcing yourself; it is about letting go of what the cave deceptively seems to offer you. Seek alternative ways to protect yourself and offer yourself the nourishment and affection you truly deserve in real love that lasts. Let go of your heart of stone and embrace a heart filled with love.

> They will say, "This land that was laid waste has become like the garden of Eden; the cities that were lying in ruins, desolate and destroyed, are now fortified and inhabited."
>
> Ezekiel 36:35 NIV

# six

# Am I a Doormat?

The wise woman builds her house, but with her own hands the foolish one tears hers down.

Proverbs 14:1 NIV

Mary was racing down an Alabama farm road at 120 miles an hour heading toward a large tree, trying to kill herself. As she approached the tree, her steering wheel locked and her car swerved, diving into a muddy ditch just beside the tree. The impact of the car hitting the ditch caused the radio to switch on, and Mary suddenly heard a voice singing, "Out from the ashes, out from the ashes, God will save you, out from the ashes." Chills went down her spine. She knew at that moment that God had supernaturally saved her from self-destruction and had some kind of purpose, other than death, for her.

As soon as Mary's husband heard the news, he rushed to the scene and took her home. As they walked in the door, the phone was ringing. A wealthy neighbor, who hadn't yet heard about the car accident, was calling. She said, "Mary, you shared with me that you have been depressed lately, so I didn't want to put off calling you any longer. I was praying, and I felt a certain urgency to call you today. I would like to pay all your expenses if you will go to the Paul Meier New Life day program in Richardson, Texas, where he and his staff can treat you during the day, for as many weeks as it takes."

"I can't accept that," Mary said.

"I insist!" said the neighbor.

At that point Mary wept and shared with her neighbor how she had just miraculously been saved by God from a suicide attempt. Her husband sat beside her weeping too. He loved her very much and couldn't understand why she continually remained depressed.

When Mary came to my (Paul's) clinic, I did a thorough psychiatric evaluation. She was a very intelligent and attractive young woman in her late thirties. She had an MBA degree and worked as an accountant at a major university in Alabama. She had a good marriage and two young children who adored her, yet she remained a "doormat woman" outside of the home.

At the university she was sexually harassed by several different men, and she always tolerated it without telling anyone, even her husband. She was also taken advantage of in many other ways. If someone didn't feel like doing his or her fair share, that person would always dump it on Mary, and she always picked up their unreasonable load without the slightest complaint. Deep inside, Mary felt like a piece of trash, like she deserved to be abused.

I discovered during my initial evaluation that she grew up in a home with no father. Her mother, to make ends meet, moved her and her older sister to a trailer park where the mother worked as a leasing agent and manager. Her mother was intelligent but passive. Mary and her older sister, Laura, were both repeatedly sexually abused by various relatives and men who lived in the trailer park. The mother knew this was going on, permitted it, and taught her daughters not to complain. "Men are just that way," she would say. As Mary got older, she and her sister took on the responsibilities of the upkeep of the trailer park while their mother slept around, abused alcohol, and became more and more irresponsible.

In their teenage years Laura and Mary went in totally different directions. By age fifteen Laura had become so disgusted with men and had such a low self-concept that she imagined that a loving and nurturing female relationship was the answer. At seventeen she abused drugs and ended up dying of a drug overdose after her female lover rejected her.

Mary, on the other hand, was invited to a church youth group by a friend at high school. She kept most of her thoughts and experiences a secret from the people at church because she was so ashamed. Being intelligent and personable, she was quickly befriended by the church's young people. After a year of attending the youth group, Mary became a Christian and developed a close personal relationship with God. She got as close as she felt comfortable with her peers but never shared with them any of her abusive experiences. She frequently thought, *If they really knew the truth about me and the trash that I am, they would certainly reject me. I am amazed that God accepts me . . . and I often have doubts about that. How* could *he accept me?*

After high school graduation Mary moved away from her mother, got a job, and put herself through college. While there, she met a wonderful young man at church and married him soon after graduating. She began her job as an accountant at the university during that time. She began working part-time when her youngest child was born.

During the initial evaluation, I counted twenty-nine different men who had sexually abused her or harassed her from the time she was six years old until age thirty-eight, and it was still continuing. She was being harassed by an employer at the university. Mary's husband knew only that her grandfather had sexually abused her as a child, but he thought it was a one-time incident and didn't know about all the other incidents. Mary had told him about her grandfather when she wanted to give her husband an explanation for her freezing up every time they tried to be physically intimate. He was very understanding and noncondemning and continued to show her genuine love, which made her feel even more guilty and ashamed of who she was. She thought, *He might reject me too if he finds out my secrets.* After all, by the age of six, she had rejected herself in many ways. Her deep self-rejection as an adult was exactly what allowed her to let people walk on her.

When people come to our day program, they stay in a hotel but come to our outpatient clinic seven hours a day for group and individual insight-oriented psychotherapy. We believe the truth sets people free. We used a variety of therapeutic techniques with Mary. For example, we put an empty chair in front of her and had her name each abuser, one at a time. We asked her to imagine each one sitting in the chair, beginning with her father, who had abandoned her. We invited her to tell him how she felt about his abandoning her as a young girl. We also encouraged her to write a letter to her deceased sister to tell her how much she missed her and how much she wishes she could still have a relationship with her. One other tool that Mary found useful was to write a letter to her mother. Before she mailed it, she talked about the contents with the therapist and a group of other clients she had been working with. She then made some modifications and sent it. In this letter she let her mother know how her mother's neglectfulness had made her feel unprotected and used.

It took four weeks of therapy for Mary to cover the bases and learn how to begin releasing her anger to God. She came to an understanding, through her faith and the insight and healing she was experiencing, that God was just and would hold each of the abusers accountable before him. She recognized that if she did not let go of her bitterness and anger, she was continuing the cycle of abuse within herself. By holding on to anger, she was letting the abusers continue to make her a victim. She had once heard a sermon about anger and revenge but was surprised at some of the specific verses we revealed to her in the day program. She hadn't been reading her Bible on a regular basis, because she didn't realize that it could be so relevant to her daily life. She discovered that Moses, speaking the words of God, said:

> Do not hate your brother in your heart. Rebuke your neighbor frankly so you will not share in his guilt. Do not seek revenge or bear a grudge against one of your people, but love your neighbor as yourself. I am the LORD.
>
> Leviticus 19:17–18 NIV

She also read: "Vengeance belongs to me; I will repay says the Lord. . . . The Lord will judge His people."[1] She hadn't connected that she had the ability to give her desire for justice over to God a long time ago. She knew she wasn't alone anymore when she came across this prayer in the Psalms: "Defend the cause of the weak and fatherless; maintain the rights of the poor and oppressed. Rescue the weak and needy; deliver them from the hand of the wicked. . . . Rise up, O God . . ." (82:3–4, 8 NIV). She realized in fact that this was what God had done when he stopped her from killing herself and provided a way for her to begin to heal.

Mary worked through the process of forgiving each abuser—something more profound than an apology or jail sentence had to be done to pay for the injustice done to her body and soul. She also took the important step of relinquishing the expectation that her father and mother would ever change. As much as she desired for them to come and engage in a loving relationship with her, she learned that she had to let go so that she could access her own ability to stand up for herself. She was the adult provider now. She, along with God and her husband and friends, could now begin to appreciate and welcome the love God had for her all along, and the love her husband, children, and friends had to add to her life.

In the day program we taught her to live her life to the full, assuming that her parents would never show up to help her do it. For her whole life she had thought her self-worth depended on their loving her and seeing value in her. She had continued in her lifelong depression because of her fantasy that someday they would love and protect her and that, when they did, she would finally feel safe and valued. It took Mary time to grieve the loss of this fantasy. In fact she cried almost every day as she went through these very difficult spiritual and psychological growth processes. By the end of four weeks, she had significantly recovered and was quite happy and at peace for the first time in her life.

I have continued to correspond with Mary for several years now and was happy to find out that she left her job at the university. She was so excited about her healing experience that she pursued a master's degree in counseling and became a licensed counselor. She now works for a mission organization that helps victims of abuse. Through her own process of healing, Mary developed an ability to empathize deeply and care for the valuable people she counsels.

## Making the Choice

The adage "You can't change another person, but you can change yourself" was quite applicable in Mary's recovery process. She was able to accept that she could not change her parents and began to change herself, giving herself respect and protection. She gave up her self-hatred and became her own loving and close friend.

If you are beginning to feel that no one pays attention to you in your own house, in your relationships with your spouse, your boyfriend or girlfriend, your children, your boss; if no one respects your boundaries, it is time to discover why you are on the floor, where you disappeared to, and what part of you still thinks that being a doormat is your place in life. When you are this low to the ground, you may think (like Mary) that suicide is the only way out of the pain. Facing your fear to stand up for yourself may *feel* impossible—it may feel more threatening than death itself—but it is *not*. Choose to reject the words of fear and cling to the words of love. Find a way to get up off the ground. Encourage yourself toward love and healing. Begin now, as Mary did in her life.

Being a doormat is destructive not only to you but also to those around you. It is time to discover what it means to pick yourself up, to stand up for yourself. Before we uncover the reasons for people agreeing to be doormats, here's a quiz to see if your life reflects any doormat characteristics.

## The Doormat Quiz

Check the characteristics that you think describe you.

___**D**oing things for others that they ought to do themselves takes up a lot of my time. I say "I'm sorry" a lot. (I say "I'm sorry" because I think everything is my fault and my responsibility.)

___**O**thers make my choices. I delay my priorities because others want my help.

___**O**thers determine my self-worth and define my identity.

___**R**ejection is what I fear most. I am controlled by the people I fear will reject me.

___**M**ad at myself for not measuring up, I have a difficult time forgiving myself.

___**A**fraid of conflict, I have a hard time saying *no* or standing up for myself.

___**T**rue love is missing from my heart. I feel like others love me for what I do.

If you checked even one of these characteristics, you have much to learn from the rest of this chapter. If you checked four or more, it is time you love yourself up to a standing position. You may have been born lying down, but you learned to stand up and walk for a reason!

The characteristics below reveal what you are choosing to give away in your choice to stay a doormat.

**D**oing things for others that they ought to do themselves.
   I give away my *praise*. I live for the praise of others.
**O**thers make my choices.
   I give away my *priorities*. Others direct my life.
**O**thers determine my self-worth and define my identity.
   I give away my *personhood*. Others determine my value.
**R**ejection is what I fear most.
   I give away my *purpose*. I reduce my purpose to fear.
**M**ad at myself for not measuring up.
   I give away my *pardon*. I am perpetually self-critical.

**A**fraid of conflict.
 I give away my *power.* I teach myself that I do not
 deserve to be powerful.
**T**rue love is missing from my heart.
 I give away my *plenty.* I relinquish the abundance I
 could experience from loving myself unconditionally.

There are many important things you give away when you
choose to stay a doormat. Some part of your brain, however,
thinks you are gaining more than you are giving, or you wouldn't
have negotiated your life in such a way. Let's discover some of
the reasons you have chosen to live as a doormat.

## Underlying Dynamics of the Doormat Lifestyle

One picture cannot encompass the entire human psyche, yet
we have found that the picture or description of the internal
dynamics of the doormat lifestyle can open our eyes to a place
of freedom and healing. By understanding the subconscious
process, we can consciously choose to let go of it! (You will
know the truth and the truth will set you free.)

The first experience most of us remember from early childhood is probably one of warmth and love.

After the initial excitement wears off and the crying begins,
the picture begins to change at home for some of us. Our parents are challenged to learn how to take responsibility for a new
life.

At the age of three and a half, Mary experienced the pain of
the abandonment of her father and the criticism and neglect
of her bitter mother. This experience taught her a new version
of love. She felt abandoned but had the conflicting feeling of
compassion for her mother, understanding that she too had
been abandoned.

Mary's new version or *distortion of love* had developed
through the following steps:

103

- A child does not want to grow up thinking her parents are bad.
- If her parents are bad (critical, neglectful, unloving), then she is without protection.
- A child, just like all of us, has a desire for protection and safety.
- To provide this safety she convinces herself that her parents are not the bad guys, but the problem is something she *is* or *has been doing*. She internalizes the message, *I am not worth my parents protecting me better, loving me more, providing for me more than they are already*. She thinks, *Maybe if I do something to make Mom or Dad happy, they will love me and I will be worth it*.
- This gives her a sense of power or control. She wants to feel like she can change herself or her behavior and, in doing so, will be able to protect herself.
- If she did not defend herself in this way, she would be looking over her shoulder all the time, never knowing when she would be hurt by "bad" parents. For many reasons, even though it may be illogical, children want to think that their parents are good and loving, and if they are not, children tend to believe that it is their fault, not the parents'.

To try to protect themselves and gain some sense of control, children internalize the "bad," thinking it is *their fault* their parents neglect them, abandon them, and treat them badly. They continue to think, *Maybe if I do something different I will get the love that I got at first*.

### *The Parental Model*

As Mary grows up, she forms her identity as a woman, modeled by her mom. As she gets older, other female role models have some influence on her understanding. Some of Mary's first ideas of being a woman that she saw in her mom included:

- Women are conveniently left and abandoned when their husbands no longer want them—or when they do something (I don't yet know what) to provoke them to leave.
- Women are made to be used and should not complain about it.
- Women are bitter at the consequences in their life and powerless to change them.
- Women have to yell and fight to get anything from others.
- Women are made to work seventy hours a week to feel important after being left by a man.

In addition to these observations, Mary learned from her older sister, Laura, the things their father had done to their mom and the names he had called her. Since both Mary's and Laura's understanding of what a woman is was formed by their understanding of their mother, they internalized their father's insults and thought, *I am a girl; my mom is a girl; I must be as bad as these words my dad called my mom.* Mary and Laura began to even more deeply question their own worth; they soon began to inwardly hate being women.

When a father or mother leaves the family, the abandoned child becomes a young man or woman who has internalized the pain, criticism, and neglect as if it had all been his or her doing. Often the young woman or teen will identify herself so much with the "bad" she has internalized that she thinks she is trash. (Men and boys do this too.) She does what she can to hide her shame but in the end believes she deserves for other people to abuse, criticize, or neglect her. She even acts that way toward herself.

She translated the message passed along to her by her parents as, *I am ugly, bad, unworthy, and undeserving of love from anyone. I must do all I can to*

- hide this part of myself that I see now (trash).
- get rid of this trash, to achieve in school and in everything so that people don't focus on the trash.

105

- become the trash that I am and allow myself to be treated as such. (It's too much of a struggle to try to prove myself otherwise.)
- find someone who will stay with me and put up with my trash—and I'll work really hard to make him happy so that maybe he will love the trash away and not add more neglect and criticism, which turn to self-hate.

It is beneficial for parents to tell a child, "This is not your fault," when they are getting a divorce; yet the words do not alter the internal feelings of abandonment, neglect, and pain that the child feels. Actions speak louder than words, so it's impossible for a child not to feel responsible when a parent leaves. They cannot otherwise make sense of the lack of their parent's presence in their daily lives.

When these girls and boys become old enough to begin dating, they often find people who are similar to their parents. At first, there is only romantic bliss. Both partners see only the potential of the love that is going to come their way from the other. They remember the initial love they had and connect with the "eternal truth" of love that is written on each of our hearts, and they long for this.

They soon find out that each person in the partnership has a storehouse of neglect and criticism inside that keeps love and closeness out. People like this often find each other because they are already familiar with this kind of person, and they try to "fix" the pain they experienced in childhood by trying to change the neglectful and critical parts of their new love interest. It feels like they are fixing their critical and neglectful parent.

We often tell ourselves, *I don't want to repeat the pattern of my parents.* However, we have already begun to learn the pattern. When we look inside ourselves, we see that we use the same tools and defenses our parents taught us and gave us. Unless we consciously work to build different skills and learn what it is to love more fully, we are doomed to repeat the same patterns we have seen and become the people we were taught we were. We choose the pattern our parents chose for themselves, because their way is familiar (family) to us. We are often loyal to the familiar.

I meet many clients who express a desire to change, yet they continue in their parents' footsteps because they feel a certain loyalty calling them. This is especially the case in abusive homes. Members of an abusive family experience a tremendous amount of betrayal. Oddly, the message to the child is, "Your father betrayed us by abandoning us; don't you betray us by creating a good life for yourself!" This is why so many people stay stuck in abusive "victim" patterns. Their family communicates to them on some level, "If you quit being a victim, you are betraying our family pattern." If the child tries to escape the common family experience, it feels like betrayal to other family members.

Imagine a child who grew up with an alcoholic father. She marries an alcoholic. She now has much in common with her mom and can commiserate with her. If the daughter had a healthy husband and healthy marriage she would begin to feel alienated from her mom, because her mom never chose to confront the situation with her alcoholic husband or do anything to change it.

Mary was fortunate to have found a spiritual and loving husband. This is very rare for those who grew up in abusive situations. Eighty-five percent of the time, when people grow up in an abusive situation in childhood, they find an abusive mate who will continue the familiar abuse. Mary wasn't abused at home, but she allowed abuse to occur at her place of employment even though she hated every moment of it.

In doing so, she was neglecting a part of herself, just as her mother had neglected her and her father had abandoned her. She also worked really hard in her adolescence and young adulthood to achieve in school. She didn't want anyone to focus on the trash she felt was so obvious inside of her. She wanted to hide it, even from herself.

### The Doormat Woman

Some men and women feel crushed when their "I'm worthless" feelings are confirmed by their first breakup of a relationship. They soon find a new person to date, and the beginning of their relationship is wonderful. The promise of love is in the air. They imagine being rescued from their family life. Both of them, however, have lots of unprotected and wounded parts. Instead of learning what it is to nurture themselves and love each other, they begin to criticize and take turns neglecting each other.

The doormat woman in this kind of relationship soon feels like the relationship is slipping. She invents creative ways to make her new boyfriend happy. She stops hanging out with her girlfriends so she can spend more time with him. She starts compromising her own personal boundaries of time, energy, and her physical body. She begins to feel a sort of desperation. She thinks that if her boyfriend leaves her, it will open up all her painful feelings of neglect and abandonment that she has stored up inside of her already. She is so afraid of the impending pain that there is no way she is going to do something to cause that floodgate to open. Instead, she starts giving in to everything her boyfriend wants. She feels more and more insecure about her physical appearance and begins starving herself, working out all the time, and taking over-the-counter, and sometimes not-over-the-counter, diet pills. Her identity begins to disappear as quickly as her weight and she begins to forget who she is. (Some women put on a lot of weight to form a "reason" that people are so rejecting and distant.) Her boyfriend soon starts cheating, while holding on to the perks of a relationship with her.

The doormat woman is willing to ignore the fact that her boyfriend is going out on her, thinking that it is better to keep him than to feel the pain of loneliness, abandonment, and rejection. Some doormat men and doormat women work all day to pay the way for their significant other to stay around the house and do nothing. These same people come home and clean the house and take care of all the bills and everything else. By doing this, the doormat-like people encourage their significant others to become even more demanding and self-absorbed.

The abusive partner in this relationship learns that he does not have to work to get anything. The doormat, by lying on the ground, is absorbing all the consequences of the other person's actions or inactions. This means that the abuser does not get the opportunity to learn from his mistakes or feel any painful consequences for his actions. Thus he has no motivation to change. When the doormat begins to stand up for herself, the person who is willing to walk on doormats will usually get really angry because the consequences for his behavior are no longer being absorbed. This is when the inevitable happens. Either he starts treating the ex-doormat worse to try to get the doormat back on the floor, or he abandons the ex-doormat and finds someone new who will put up with his behavior. When this happens the ex-doormat is free! The abuser didn't really want a relationship with a person who had her own opinions and thoughts. He wanted a doormat, and you can buy those at the store!

### *Summing Up the Doormat Lifestyle*

Someone who grows up feeling loved and respected by parents will usually connect with his or her own support group of loving friends. If this person dates someone who treats him or her with disrespect, he or she immediately breaks off that relationship—and ought to be applauded for doing so.

The doormat person, on the other hand, treats himself or herself like trash, because that's what the person feels he or she already is inside. And yet this same doormat person continually stays bitter and angry with his or her spouse, father, mother, and others for their treatment. Out of desperation, he or she puts up with abusive dates and ends up married to an abuser. If the abuser repents and changes into a loving mate, the doormat will usually divorce the changed mate and marry another abuser, remaining totally ignorant of the true reason for doing so and inventing false reasons in order to hide the truth that he or she is continuing to choose the victim role.

We learned in the previous chapter how we sometimes try to offer ourselves protection by running to caves. We can also think we are protecting ourselves by lying down as doormats, because we think that if we are compliant we will get the love we want so desperately. When women want to protect themselves from their unrequited longing for love and also don't want their boundaries invaded (by being a doormat), they sometimes create their own kinds of escape through their body. They treat their body like a doormat. Some starve themselves, a picture of the malnourishment they have felt for so long (lack of love from either or both mother and father); then they think *they* are in control. *I am not the victim here, because I am the one choosing to neglect myself through food.* They believe they have two options: Continue to feel awful for being neglected by their parents or be the powerful one and neglect themselves. Starving themselves also serves to regress them into a childlike place, where they form a genderless body. They feel like this genderlessness will protect them from invaders.

We move to various kinds of extreme ways in our efforts to get love for ourselves. We fail to see that love all along waits for us to take hold of it. Think about whether the pattern you have been engaging in is working for you. I mean really working. Are you getting the love you want? Whether it is being a doormat, confirming the message, "I am trash and do not deserve love," or running from everyone because you are tired of being stepped on, it is time to move on and take hold of love. Learn to stand up for yourself. Learn to connect. You deserve it.

In the last section of this chapter we will look at why we deserve this kind of love.

## Who We Were Created to Be

I have met women who run the show at work and tell everyone where to go. At home, though, the process is reversed. They feel unseen, unheard, disrespected, unprotected, very much like a doormat that people leave their dirt on. They feel like they are responsible for everyone else's pain while no one cares to embrace theirs or nurture them in their hurting and empty places. But doormat people, when they stand up for themselves, can inspire others to care about them.

It is so important to choose to be gentle and discover what our core beliefs are deep inside. It is important that we locate the voices that tell us we are "bad girls" (or "bad boys") whenever we get up off the ground. When as children we dreamed of the future, we dreamed of being princesses or princes, worthy of a whole kingdom. We dreamed of a fairy godmother rescuing us from being treated like a doormat.

As children we felt that our abusive situations couldn't change unless an adult happened to notice and intervene. Many of us adults still dream of the day we will magically become princesses or the day our fairy godmother (or our repentant mother) will show up. We wish on stars but do not give ourselves the opportunity to make our dreams come true. Mary got used to being abused and, after a while, believed it was inevitable. She learned to zone out and disconnect herself from the situation. She never encouraged abuse, but abusers can sense which people will be doormats and which ones will fight for themselves. Abusers were attracted to Mary because they could see in her eyes that she was too passive to put up a fight.

If we wish to be treated like princes and princesses, sons and daughters of a good King, worthy of respect, this is how we are to treat ourselves. We model this new way of being to those around us, who perhaps do not know this model yet. This does not mean that we are to treat ourselves as if everyone must worship us, but to learn, instead, from the very stories we read to our children. Here is a quote to remember from a classic fairy tale: "The truest princess is just the one who loves all her brothers and sisters best, and who is most able to do them good by being humble towards them."[2] Being humble is different from letting people walk on you. It is said that Moses was a very humble man, yet he stood up to the pharaoh of Egypt so that God's chosen people could be rescued from living as doormats.

In C. S. Lewis's Narnia Chronicles God is represented as the Great Emperor Beyond the Sea. Aslan, the lion, King of the Beasts, enters the story as the Great Emperor's son, redeemer of all the talking animals and humans in the land. If God truly is our Father, King, and Creator, and we are his beloved children, then we are all princes and princesses. Our job here on earth is to discover what it is to fulfill that role, to truly reflect his beautiful creation within us and to respect the beauty we see within others. This is no mere fantasy or story but the true story of our lives.

During Mary's time at our clinic, we shared Psalm 139 with her. In that chapter King David wrote that God designed us in our mother's womb. That passage tells us that when we fell asleep last night, God was thinking about us personally. When we woke up this morning, he was still thinking about us. He thinks about us so many times each day that we can't even count them. With one arm he hugs us and with the other arm he leads us to various healing experiences.

When Mary's steering wheel locked, God was there. When "Out from the Ashes" was on the car radio, God was there. When a wealthy friend called her and offered to pay for her to come to the clinic, God was there. And when we as therapists put our arms around Mary and gave her a hug, God was there hugging Mary, using our arms. God is with us as we begin to care for and nurture ourselves.

When we look at the original Greek text for Ephesians 2:10, we discover the word *poiema,* which is the root of our word *poem.* The concept of "God's poem" is often missed by the usual translation of this verse, which uses the word *workmanship.* Here is the verse from the New Living Translation: "For we are God's *masterpiece.* He has created us anew in Christ Jesus, so that we can do the good things he planned for us long ago."

We are living creations of God. Each of us is a poem searching for harmony and rhythm, a masterpiece wanting to be created with love and excellence by our loving Creator. We are encouraged in the Holy Scripture to "put on the new self, which in the likeness of God has been created in righteousness and holiness of the truth" (Eph. 4:24 NASB). "Put on the new self who is being renewed to a *true knowledge according to the image of the One* who created him" (Col. 3:10 NASB, emphasis added). Since God is love and we are made in his image, our best guess is that he is continually inviting us to receive *more* love, to be transformed so that fear is released and love has its room to grow us spiritually.

We are reminded so vividly of this concept of being living poems, masterpieces in progress, transformed by the loving hand of God, in Rilke's *Letters to a Young Poet:*

> How could we forget those ancient myths that stand at the beginning of all races, the myths about dragons that at the last moment are transformed into princesses? Perhaps all the dragons in our lives are princesses who are only waiting to see us act, just once, with beauty and courage. Perhaps everything that frightens us is, in its deepest essence, something helpless that wants our love.[3]

Although there are many individual factors involved in how we form our understanding of ourselves, we can begin with a framework we saw in Mary, with which many of us will relate. Our goal is to understand how we have viewed ourselves in the past and why. What are our core beliefs and perceptions of ourselves and others? These are the ideas we are invested in that keep us stuck in a doormat position. These are the lies we hold on to that teach us to live in fear, keeping us trapped in the belief that we are as ugly and unlovable as a dragon. Mary believed the lies that (1) she was worthless, (2) abuse was inevitable, (3) she was powerless to stand up to abusers, and (4) death was the only way out. When she discovered the truth and grieved her losses, the truth set her free. She re-membered her true identity and recovered herself in the knowledge that she was a child of a king, the God of love, who was all the time working in her and through her and outside of her to remind her to stand up to fear and embrace love and self-respect.

## Wrapping Up

We have discovered there are many factors that lead a woman or a man to feel that she or he is a doormat and deserves nothing more than to be treated as one. Some men and women fight very hard to prove that they are not doormats. It is truly when we begin to cultivate an understanding of ourselves as created by God, designed for a purpose, poems to be discovered, that we find freedom. We discover that we do not have to prove to others that we are not trash, because we inwardly know we aren't. We do not have to be afraid of rejection or abandonment, because we know how to nurture and love ourselves and find others who will share this same kind of love with us. We will not abandon ourselves. Neither will God abandon us. We do not tear our houses down with our own hands but build them up. We do not hide behind false facades but build our houses on a solid foundation and learn what it is to let go of the blame we have accepted for so long. It is time we take out the trash ourselves—the trash that was not ours to begin with—and respond to God by living like his adult children.

# seven

# What Do You Expect?

For a person, for an animal, indeed for any living being, there is neither logic nor meaning in the word "freedom" because all our lives are limited by many constraints. And yet if a person understands himself as a spiritual being, he cannot even speak about not being free: the idea of not being free cannot be applied to the notions of intellect, conscience, and love.

Leo Tolstoy

What do you get from expectations? Where is freedom in expectations? When you take a second look, you see that when expectations are unmet, disappointment follows. When you expect something, you wait or stay. In other words, when you expect someone to show up in your life and take care of something for you, you wait for that person. This means you stay stuck in one place until that person shows up, *if* that person shows up. Your choice to hold on to expectations takes away your freedom to move. We move to free ourselves when we take the time to stop and listen to what our expectations have to reveal to us. In this chapter you will learn how expectations are a mask, covering up the communication of your deepest desires.

Earlier we learned that children have to wait. As a child you had little choice. You sat in your crib and waited for the milk to show up, for someone to hold you, someone to change you, and someone to keep you clean. As an adult you have the ability and thus the freedom to walk, drive, get a job, buy your food, bathe yourself, and, most important, surround yourself with loving people. So, then, why do we choose to go backwards and wait around expecting others to parent us? Why do we invite disappointment into our daily lives?

In expectation you wait in hope that others will change. You put on hold the living of your life, the fulfilling of your purpose, the loving that you could be embracing and giving back to the world, while you wait for that person or those people (whoever they are for you) to show up. When you put yourself in a waiting position, you are passive and have *no idea* when the "good" will come your way or *if* it ever will!

Before we learn how to let go of expectations, it is important that we understand what makes expecting so appealing to us. There has to be something attractive to putting our lives on hold, waiting for others, and then resenting them when they don't show up to take care of us or love us the way we desire or we would not do it. There is always a payoff of some kind, no matter how much pain or how high the cost. We choose not to change because we do not want to let go of the results we are getting now. Take a moment to complete this sentence to discover what the appeal is for you individually:

I like waiting in expectation for others because

_____.

Now that you understand one way you are attracted to expectations, let's explore what waiting and expecting look like and some of the "payoffs" we may get from staying stuck.

## What Waiting Looks Like

We see this waiting game illustrated beautifully in the lyrics of Bob Marley's reggae song "Waiting in Vain." He sings about waiting to see if the woman he has been waiting for, for three years, is going to reciprocate his love. His eyes burn with tears as he waits for her, telling her that he does not want to wait in vain. He does not know if the woman he is waiting for will ever requite his love. He waits in expectation, yet he asks her to release him, to give him a clue as to *when* or *if* she will ever love him. (He also indicates that he is just about ready to stop waiting around for her!)

In love songs all the way from Bob Marley to the Beatles, Beach Boys, and Billie Holiday, we can see a picture of the singer taking all of his/her spiritual longings for real love and wrapping them up into a hope or expectation that the one person he or she is pining for will show up and fill the void completely. Longing is romantic. We believe that we will be magically freed from the dungeon of ourselves if only the fair princess comes to draw us out, if only the prince in shining armor comes riding up on his white stallion. To wish to be released from the dungeon of self is a true and noble wish. To wait for a chair to bring you the key would be foolish. I am convinced that no one expresses this longing for love better than Søren Kierkegaard in his February 2, 1839, diary entry:

> Oh, blind god of Love! You who see into our hidden recesses, will you reveal love to me? Shall I find here below what I seek, shall I experience the Conclusion drawn from all my life's eccentric premises, am I to hold you in my arms—or do you order me to be on my way?
>
> Have you gone before me, my *yearning*, are you beckoning to me, transfigured, from another world? Oh, I will cast off everything to become light enough to follow you.[1]

These longings are beautiful, though still merely glimpses of *true love*'s capabilities:

> Eros is in a sense right to make this promise. . . . In one high bound it has overleaped the massive wall of our selfhood; it has made appetite itself altruistic, tossed personal happiness aside as a triviality and planted interests of another in the centre of our being. Spontaneously and without effort we have fulfilled the law [towards one person] by loving our neighbor as our-

selves. *It is an image, a foretaste, of what we must become to all if Love Himself rules in us without a rival.*[2]

C. S. Lewis writes here of our expectations of love. The Greek language has several words for love. *Eros* often implies being in love in the romantic sense. The fullness of love we feel in the "love is blind" romantic stage is a picture of the love that we want to experience for all of eternity. Lewis describes it as an appetizer. He is saying that the more we invite real Love, God himself, for God is Love, to teach us what love is, the more we experience this heavenly love. We cannot fake this love. It is real, true, genuine, and deep.

We often expect the feeling of being in love to be the same as this deep love that we learn from God and want for eternity. When being in love does not turn out to be this deep love that we expected, we often become sad and disillusioned about the person we love or about love in general. Lewis here sheds light on what happens when we think that the "being in love" feeling will magically cause us to continue loving the person we hold dear—when we expect our initial feeling to cause the love to last without effort on our part.

> The couple whose marriage will certainly be endangered . . . are those who have idolised Eros. They thought he [Eros] had the power and truthfulness of a god. *They expected the mere feeling would do for them, and permanently, all that was necessary.* When this expectation is disappointed they throw blame on Eros or, more usually, on their partners. In reality, however, Eros, having made his gigantic promise and shown you a glimpse what its performance would be like, has "done his stuff." . . . *It is we who must labour to bring our daily life into even closer accordance with what the glimpses have revealed.*[3]

It is in understanding this concept that we can appreciate our longings. Our expectations reveal we want something. When we understand this something that we are longing for, we can go about satisfying it in a real and fulfilling way. We can appreciate our longings and be active about responding to them, instead of waiting for someone else to do the work for us. If we expected a jelly bean to fill our craving for dinner, we would be left hungry and angry at the jelly bean for disappointing us. The jelly bean was ill-equipped to do the job that a healthy dinner would do. When we seek the dinner first, we free ourselves to enjoy the jelly bean afterward. We won't be frustrated and upset because we set up the order of the dinner and the jelly bean in accordance with the true purpose that they were equipped to meet.

There is a longing deep within us that can be filled only by God. We read in Proverbs 19:22 (NIV): "What a man desires is unfailing love." No one but God has perfect, unfailing love. We wonder if we can truly access this love in our daily lives. We pursue this love and learn about it when we form unbreakable bonds. The very idea that we have this desire within us indicates there is a promise that we will have satisfaction. God made the desire; he inscribed it within us. God is not a sadist who wants us to long for something our whole lives without the chance of being fulfilled (though we may think that by the way our own parents kept us "hanging").

One of my favorite verses that teaches us to let go of our fears of "wasted expectations" or "waiting in vain" in our relationship with God is found in the apostle Paul's writings:

> For while we are in this tent, we groan and are burdened, because we do not wish to be unclothed but to be clothed with our heavenly dwelling. . . . Now it is God who has made us for this very purpose and has given us the Spirit as a deposit, guaranteeing what is to come. Therefore we are always confident.
>
> 2 Corinthians 5:4–6 NIV

As Christians, we have Jesus already. We have the Holy Spirit dwelling within us at this very moment. This is a true reality for those of faith to grasp. This is another door we have within us that we may have hardly recognized or opened on our own. Remember what Jesus said, that if we had faith as small as a mustard seed, we could move a whole mountain into the sea! We read in the passages of the New Testament that the Holy

119

Spirit of God, who is in us, is the same Spirit who raised Jesus from the dead. If we knew fully what that meant in our daily lives, we would truly comprehend that we lack nothing. Our spiritual self has access now to all we ever need spiritually. We press on to know his unfailing love!

It is my understanding that all of these deep longings for unfailing love are hidden below our "daily expectations." This is why some of us may not even be aware that these deeper longings are there. We get distracted and caught up in the daily expectations we place on life—and those we take on by others. Some of the above ideas may not make a lot of sense to you right now, because we could go on learning about these things for our whole life. Here in this chapter we are still *detecting* what gets in our way of love. One of the main things we see over and over again in our office and in our own lives are those "daily expectations" that have not yet been uncovered and understood.

We often put these everyday expectations on others—our employees, employers, spouse, children, friends, and even God. We choose to play the waiting game with them. Sometimes we wait for our children to parent us or fill us up with what we feel we are missing. We end up having a long list of people we resent, including ourselves, when these expectations aren't met. Sometimes God ends up on that list too, because he often doesn't run the world the way we want him to.

We are taught in Ephesians 3:20 that God is able to do immeasurably more in our lives than we could possibly begin to imagine or ask of him. That does not mean that God will do everything *for* us. In Proverbs 8 we are encouraged to actively seek wisdom as if searching for gold. We do not just wake up to find wisdom under our pillow (as much as we would like that). To expect God to do the work for us, while we just wait for it to be done, is to ask God to grow up for us, to learn the eternal truths that we were meant to learn ourselves. He already knows them. For us to ask him to give us a list of things he wants us to "do" in some rote fashion and also then to ask him to make it all happen is to ask God to take away the very freedom and individuality he gave us when he created us. He wants to freely give us his love and for us to take hold of the true under-standing of things; yet there is still some initiative to be taken on our part if we truly want these things.

Step 2 of the Twelve Steps in Alcoholics Anonymous reflects the concept we are talking about. Bill Wilson developed a process to give addicts a chance to take hold of true healing. (All the other doctors of his day had practically given up on finding any effective "cure" for alcoholism.) Step 2 says: "We came to believe that a Power greater than ourselves could restore us to sanity."

It is important for us to ask ourselves if what we *expected* to fulfill us, outside of God, has in fact filled us. We wanted our addictions to give us enough pleasure to eradicate all hints of loneliness we held within. When we learn how to let go of our expectations in addictions, things, or people that will not *ulti-mately* fulfill us and begin to pursue that which will, we will feel full and will then unlock our ability to enjoy the relation-ships and activites in our lives we were meant to enjoy. In this same way, when we look to God, a spiritual being higher in intelligence and greater in love than ourselves, we can begin to find true wisdom, restoration of our sanity, and order in our lives.

I like the wording in step 2: "a Power . . . *could* restore us to sanity." It implies that it is up to us to take hold of this possi-bility and initiate action. This is the freedom that God gives us out of his grace. It is important, on your quest for wholeness, to discover the doors to freedom that wait for you when you let go of expectations.

## Expectations and Desires

When we have expectations, we are saying, "I expect this to get done or I will be disappointed." When we look up the word *disappointed* in the dictionary, we find a clue. *Disappointed* means "defeated in expectation or hope; (obsolete) not ade-quately equipped." How fortunate we are that they still put obso-lete definitions in the dictionary! The definition "not adequately equipped" gives us insight into what is going on. We are disappointed when someone or something does not measure up to what we were hoping for. It means that someone or something was *not adequately equipped* to meet our expectation. In your daily life it may look more like this: "Billy, I expect you to bring home a trophy from your soccer game today." The underlying message to your son Billy may look something like this: "You will make Mommy and Daddy really proud and make our whole family feel better about ourselves if you achieve in this way."

It is one thing to have a *goal* for Billy to play to the best of his ability; it is another thing altogether for all your hopes of feeling like a "good mother" or a "good father" to be resting on poor Billy's bringing home a trophy. No matter what kind of an athlete Billy is, he is not adequately equipped to fulfill that expectation. Billy is *not* inadequate. But when we expect him to fulfill a role or purpose that he was *not* made to fulfill, we get defeated, deflated, discouraged, and frustrated. We set ourselves up to get frustrated, and we set Billy up to feel like a failure throughout his life every time he doesn't bring home various "trophies."

Let's listen in to a phone conversation to see another way we are like this in our everyday lives:

Chandra: Oh, Meg, I told you about Raymond, didn't I? I'm planning on marrying that guy, Raymond, from my church; he just seems so perfect for me.

Meg: But didn't you just meet him, Chandra?

Chandra: Well, yes. But that was two months ago! He is just perfect for me, Meg! I knew that God would send someone along to heal me of all the sadness I have from my divorce from David.

Meg: Chandra, it's only been two months. . . . I mean, you know that I want to be excited for you and your life, but I don't know about this.

Chandra: Hmm . . . well, you know how I felt after David. He was always just so mad at me for everything. Raymond just does everything I want and thinks everything about me is great.

Meg: I am so glad you found someone who is kind to you. . . . Hmm, wasn't David nice in the very beginning? What if Raymond changes or something? We can hardly know people in two months.

Chandra: Well . . . maybe I'm just wanting Raymond to come and save the day or something. I still find myself crying a lot over the mess in my first marriage.

Chandra and Meg continued talking for hours, as we women will do from time to time! We can see in this brief part of the conversation that Chandra was hoping that Raymond, some-one she hardly knew, would heal all the wounded parts left in her soul from her previous marriage. Even if she had known him longer, he wouldn't be any better equipped to heal every-thing broken in Chandra. It is true that loving relationships can work in us to heal lots of areas that were broken in the past, but Raymond was not adequately equipped, nor could he be adequately equipped here on this earth, to meet the kind of expectations that Chandra had for him. We are all like Chan-dra at times. She wasn't even aware how "loaded" her expec-tations for Raymond were. I can see them introducing them-selves to each other:

Chandra: Hi, I'm Chandra and I am so glad to meet you. I am expecting you to heal all the broken places left over in my soul from my childhood and my previous marriage, just all the places where I didn't have enough love.

Raymond: Great! It's nice to meet you, Chandra, because I am expecting you to heal all those same kinds of places in me, except, did I mention I have been married twice? So good luck!

This seems like a funny example, and yet over time a relation-ship built on this false premise can turn into a relationship filled with much anger and resentment. Underneath the anger is sad-ness and unhealed, unloved places in people that often con-tinue to go unloved and unhealed. We just think, *I got the wrong guy. He was too inadequate to heal these places, so I will just find someone else.* Or sometimes we think, *She was just not good looking enough for me. I never felt good about myself around her.* No person is equipped to *make you* feel good about yourself. It doesn't matter if the woman is a six-foot-two-inch supermodel. If you feel like you do not have much worth inside, she is not going to change that.

I (Cheryl) was at a beauty salon here in Southern California when I overheard an older woman next to me talking loudly about how she *had to* get plastic surgery on her face and body or her husband said he would leave her. She said it so matter-of-factly, she must have thought it was a reasonable expectation. I didn't know her and I wasn't her psychologist, so I couldn't very well just stand up and ask her, "What are you thinking?" But I left feeling sad for her and for her husband.

We all have inappropriate expectations of ourselves and others, which, in the end, set us up for disappointment and disillusionment. We desire to be loved, healed, valued, secure, safe, listened to, and unconditionally accepted. In the ideal life, parents supply these desires to their children through their words and actions. In the real world, since most parents are not perfect no matter how hard they try, much of what we desired was lacking. This is why we went over re-membering yourself and recovering your purpose in chapters 2 and 3, because we realize that we cannot teach ourselves a true and perfect idea of love from an imperfect source. We look to God and the eternity that is written on our hearts, the eternal truths we find there. Unfortunately, we are not perfect at discerning these truths either! So choose to be full of grace and gentle with yourself in this process of discovery.

Here is how we know we are operating on expectations. We say:

"You have to do this . . ." / "I have to . . ."
"I need you to do this . . ." / "I need to do . . ."
"I expect you to . . ." / "I expect this from myself . . ."

Remember, as a child, we needed everything. We would die unless our parents, or some other older person, provided us with what we needed. Children by their nature are in need and learn through the process of growing up how to care for self and others.

In expectations, unless we consciously teach our brain otherwise, we revert to our childhood way of thinking: "I *need* Raymond to heal all these places in me or I will die."

It often progresses more like this: "I *need* to get plastic surgery or my husband will leave me. I need to keep my husband around because, if he leaves, I won't feel loved anymore. I need to feel loved, or I will feel worthless. I need to feel worth something, or else why am I here on this earth? I need to feel like I have worth. I need to feel loved. I need my husband to be the one to love me; thus, I need to get the plastic surgery my husband is expecting of me!"

Let's stop for a minute and think about this woman's alternatives to plastic surgery. See them in your mind. Unless you consciously choose to expand your model of choices, you will end up thinking in a similar fashion. The untrue part of her thinking is where she says to herself, *My husband is the only incoming source of love that I can access.* It may be true that her husband is the only incoming source of love that she *has accessed,* but it is not the only incoming source of love that she *can access.* God created us to live in community, with his love, with others' love, and with our own ability to give love to ourselves. (We are also made to give love to God and to others.)

We give away our power to access all the love in the world and provide for ourselves when we live expecting others to do this for us. We also give away our power when we accept their expectations, when we agree to try to fill the role of God for them because we want to please them. We may feel really important for a while that we are in charge of making someone else feel good, but when we do not turn out to be God, the expecting person can sometimes get really mad. Look at how mad we get at God when he doesn't do all the work for us that we expect him to do! He is perfect in love, and we still get mad at him because of our imperfect understanding of love.

C. S. Lewis wrote about this in his book aptly titled *The Problem of Pain.*

> What would really satisfy us would be a God who said of anything we happened to like doing "What does it matter so long as they are contented?" We want, in fact, not so much a Father in Heaven as a grandfather in heaven—a senile benevolence who, as they say, "liked to see young people enjoying themselves," and whose plan for the universe was simply that it might be truly said at the end of each day, "a good time was had by all." Not many people, I admit, would formulate a theology in precisely those terms: but a conception not very different lurks at the back of many minds. I do not claim to be an exception: I should very much like to live in a universe which was governed on such lines. But since it is abundantly clear that I don't, and since I have reason to believe, nevertheless, that God is Love, I conclude that my conception of love needs correction.[4]

## Real Needs and Perceived Needs

You may get tired of this saying, but it is true nevertheless: "You will know the truth and the truth will set you free." When we as adults treat our wants as needs, we are operating under a false premise. When we think beyond what we saw modeled to us, we find that there is truth, or a greater truth, than our parents taught us. You will know it is a greater truth when you see yourself living a greater life!

When a child begins to scream in a toy store, demanding the newest toy, the parents give in, wanting to fulfill a "need" for their child. In so doing, they are training their child that a want *does* equal a need. When these children become adults, their perception of needs continues: "I need this expensive car or else I will die!"

Do you hear yourself saying to your spouse, "I have all these needs, and you are not doing anything about them"? Let's look at how loaded that statement is and what you can do to learn and grow from it.

A *need* implies necessity. When we think we have a need, we are thinking somewhere inside, *Unless you meet this need of mine, I am afraid I will die!* This means that you think your spouse (or some other person) *must* fulfill your need—it is an imperative. He or she is given no choice in the matter. Your survival depends on the other person's doing what you just told him or her you need. But often what we think we need is really just something we want. We treat our *wants* as *needs* all the time without realizing it.

God gave us freedom of choice for a reason. When we take away that freedom from others and from ourselves through our expectations and needs, we take away joy. We take away the opportunity of others and of ourselves to make a choice, to freely engage in loving. When we *agree* with an expecting person that their wants are indeed needs, then we feel obligated to do what they expect, even if we are inadequately equipped to take care of their expectation. When we take away choice, we smother the possibilities of love that were waiting to be awakened. When we treat our wants as needs, we are living life in a panic, frantically trying to take care of needs before we "die" or we cause others to "die."

When we wrongly treat our wants as needs, we are often more impulsive and thoughtless with our decisions. Because we thought we were responding to a need instead of recognizing it as a want, we take shortcuts that we later regret. For instance, a woman feels unloved and she immediately thinks, *I need love from my husband.* She then begins thinking, *My husband is not giving me the love I need, so I will go have an affair with some husband-substitute so I can get the love that I require to live on.* This is an extreme example of how our perceived needs can urge us to pursue fulfillment in ways that inevitably bring us unhappiness instead of the joy we seek.

If you grew up resenting all the ways your parents didn't give you love and continue as an adult expecting them to change and resenting them for not doing so, you will most likely carry out this same pattern with your spouse. If you do not make an effort to stop it (as we will explore in the next chapter), you repeat the cycle of expectation and resentment. You withhold love from yourself by waiting for your parents because you continue to think they are the only source from which you can derive love and worth. As long as you wait, you do not give this love to yourself. Often you find someone else who is also waiting for his or her parents. Then you can both stay mad at your parents, withhold love from yourselves, and resent your partner for not giving you the love you are still waiting for from your parents.

To learn how to love and give love to yourself, you do not have to wait for your parents or your spouse. What if the woman's husband in the "affair" example were cold and distant? It is true, she does become cold and distant to herself when she waits around for him to change. She does not realize it consciously, because she is overwhelmed by her anger at her husband for not taking care of her need. She soon realizes that she is also being cold and distant to herself by looking to a *quick fix* to fill her "need."

Once she recognizes she *wants* love, then and only then can she do something about it! As an adult she is able to provide these things for herself. Now she can learn (for those of us who did not have strong "loving" examples, it is a process of consciously learning) how to love and receive love. She can rise to the occasion and really learn what it is to provide for herself.

This does not mean the "unloved woman" is an island. It means she can reach out, create some consistent and deep female friendships, go to church, meet with others who have similar hobbies, and pursue countless other options. She does not have to act out of desperation. We will not die, unless we sit and do not begin to learn what it is to nourish, love, and provide for ourselves.

This is why people become suicidal. They are so mad at their parents or others for not showing up to love them that they are mad enough to kill. They do not feel worthy of love. Because no one else is showing up to love them, they think: *I will show them*. They take their own life when all along they had the ability to access a limitless love from God and countless other sources of love in a community of people, including themselves.

## The Trap of False "Needs"

In chapter 4 we explored the hidden ways we put our lives on hold and remain immobilized by waiting for someone else to change. We expect changes in their lives so our own growth can take place. This seems natural to us, yet when we take a second look at it, we see that we have rendered ourselves helpless and are bound to resent those we expect to take care of our "needs."

You may have difficulty at first discerning within yourself what a need is and what a want is. You may have friends and a significant other who tell you everything is a need. They expect you to take care of them in ways they are not taking care of themselves.

We often think that to "help" others is the most loving thing we can do. The word *help* means "to rescue, as if from death." If someone is really at death's door, it is wise to offer assistance. Sometimes, however, we think we are helping when we are really making the other person or ourselves more dependent and weak. If we try to *help* a butterfly as it is struggling to break free of its cocoon, we will actually be hurting the butterfly. The butterfly's wings are strengthened in the struggle to open its protective covering. If we keep the butterfly from strengthening its wings, we have taken away the butterfly's only chance of survival. How were we to know that we were destroying the very life we were trying to help? If we are not intentional and conscious of our daily interactions with others, how are we to know if we are truly living in accordance with love?

## Finding Your True Desire

If you have struggles with any of the expectation ideas we brought up in this chapter, seek truth, seek healing. It is important to move toward setting goals for yourself instead of waiting in expectation for others. Begin listening to your desires and learning how to provide for yourself. If your daily life is dramatically affected by your personal dynamics, get therapy for yourself, go to a church, talk to a pastor or wise teacher who shares your faith. Think of people you know who could be community for you. You deserve to be loved.

If anyone tells you, "You are selfish for going to therapy, for thinking about why you do the things you do, for considering your ways, for working on self-improvement," you do not have to take that in as truth. It is odd that the happy people are more often those who take the time to learn how to respect themselves and nurture themselves. They are thus more able to reach out to others and generously interact with them. They have the ability to provide for themselves. The self-absorbed people are often the ones who stay in victim positions, unwilling to change, passively waiting for someone to come and provide for them and resentful and bitter when they don't. When we learn how to nurture ourselves and shift our focus, we gain the wisdom and understanding that there are others in the world besides ourselves who can benefit from the nurturing skills we have developed.

When we neglect and deprive ourselves, we create patterns inside of us like those of an addict. We cycle through indulging ourselves then neglecting or starving ourselves. We think that to "indulge" is the only way to feel full. In doing this we ensure that we are constantly in pain. (Imagine starving yourself and then gorging on honey. How sick to your stomach you would become!) For many it is not that they intended to be self-absorbed but that they do not feel like they deserve to be nurtured. They do not treat themselves to self-care. Then they resent that they have been so long neglected, so they overindulge in something seemingly pleasurable. Thus they are in pain from the neglect and in pain from the consequences of overindulging.

As a psychologist and a psychiatrist, we cannot do what only God can do. We can be loving to you. We can teach you what we have learned through working with people in pain and thinking about the patterns we all engage in. We can encourage you to learn how to let go of expectations so that you can take care of yourself. If you know how to access God's limitless love, you know how to be loving to yourself, and you know how to form a loving community, then you will naturally long to share this love with others. You will be overflowing with love!

Behind your expectation you will always find a hidden agenda; usually this agenda has to do with a desire for unfailing love of some kind. The exercise we have created in this chapter is made so that you can discover what it is you truly desire.

I am constantly amazed in therapy sessions when we move to the topic of expectations. Expectations can be beacons of light on your wounded soul. Your expectations hold many secrets. As I work with patients through this exercise, we are often surprised by what we unearth.

### The Secret to Unlocking Your Unmet Expectations: Listening to the Secrets They Reveal

Write down ten expectations you have of others—your spouse, boyfriend, girlfriend, friend, boss, employee, and others.

1.
2.
3.
4.
5.
6.
7.
8.
9.
10.

Now write a list of ten expectations you have (or had before reading the chapter) for yourself.

1.
2.
3.
4.
5.
6.
7.
8.
9.
10.

Now look at both of your lists and discover what parts of yourself are demanding attention. Make a new list of your wants, making them as specific as possible. List ways you can satisfy those wants yourself by mobilizing your resources. For example, if I expect my husband to show up for dinner on time, my want is to feel respected, valued, and to have consistency. Discover first how you can become more consistent, valuing, and respectful toward yourself. Another way I can choose to give myself what I want is by inviting my husband to dinner. If he repeatedly does not show up or call ahead, then I make plans to have dinner without him. The main change that is necessary is taking back your investment in allowing your husband to define your worth by his actions. His actions are his own, and with those actions he invites consequences. It is not your job to punish him but to tell him ahead of time that you choose not to continue waiting for him. If it is reasonable for the family to have a later dinner on a consistent basis when he could be there, then you can negotiate that. If he continues not to show up, then you set up boundaries that are self-respecting.

God did not intend for us to treat people as if the world revolved around them! That is not love. We are each his children, called to know a deeper definition of love than walking on eggshells. Begin to empower yourself and enrich your life through understanding what it is you truly long for.

When we discern what our own wants and needs are and begin to make goals for ourselves instead of expecting others to take care of us, we are doing as Jesus said: "First remove the plank from your own eye, and then you will see clearly to remove the speck from your brother's eye" (Matt. 7:5). You are attending to the plank of wood you have in your own eye—this is not about self-condemnation but discovering what is still lacking—then learning how to become more whole. You see what that board is blocking you from and you remove that board. As you eliminate these hindrances to understanding yourself, there are fewer barriers between you and the truth. You gain clarity of mind. You become more loving and more open to seek others for connection instead of pursuing the pattern of expectation, rescue, and resentment.

You cannot change another person, but you can begin to take steps toward really listening to and caring for yourself.

# Part 3

# CONNECTION

We explore how to cultivate connection and commit to the process on a daily basis.

We move to experiencing genuine love and deeper connection.

We practice the art of loving and being loved.

# eight

# Preparing for Limitless Love

Man finds it hard to get what he wants, because he does not want the best; God finds it hard to give, because He would give the best, and man will not take it.

George MacDonald

Now we get to move to the fun part of connecting! You have determined your direction—to move toward love. You have detected your internal ways-of-being and self-messages that were keeping love out. Now you have the opportunity to invite the deeper love and connection into your life. There is one catch to this process, however. In order to invite the greater love in, it is important to make room for it.

Imagine if your favorite furniture store or car dealership called you and said, "We've got one million dollars' worth of goods for you, and we can deliver them whenever you are ready." The problem is that the furniture you already have in your house or the cars already in your garage are taking up all the room. They won't just disappear on their own, and you must make room for the new—selling some, giving some away, or finding an organization that can make use of your old cars and furniture.

The landscape of your soul is similar to your house. Your self-destructive patterns and sense of worthlessness take up lots of room. When you let go of the unloving parts that you have tightly held on to before, you make room for an infinite amount of love. An odd thing happens when we make room for love. More rooms appear that love can flow into. More love flows out from parts of ourselves we didn't even know we had. With love, our hearts grow bigger and bigger, whereas with destruction, our hearts grow smaller and smaller, leaving little room to know or feel love at all.

Imagine, then, that the car dealership arrives with a million dollars' worth of cars and finds plenty of room in your garage for them. Then they say, "Every month we are going to come back with another million dollars' worth of cars for you." And every month, sure enough, they show up, and your garage suddenly expands. It starts looking like the parking lot at the mall. The funny thing is, you can invite all your friends who are ready for new cars themselves. You are not worried about running out; you have more cars than you would use in a whole lifetime.

Love works the same way. God doesn't say to us, "You cannot have love unless you meet this condition." It is more like the quote at the beginning of this chapter: God has all the love to give, but if we do not make room for him or his love, where can he put it in our lives? Remember, the nature of love is not force. Evil can be forced on us; love, real love, cannot.

The process of moving on to healthy connecting is found in learning how to *let go*. This may seem like a simple process, yet we have found it is *most crucial* to psychological growth and happiness. When we let go of

living for others' approval

the unavailable others we have been running to

false guilt and condemnation

our fears that falsely promise to "protect" us

the parents in our minds that tell us, "Don't change!"

136

the resentment that keeps us from intimacy
expectations
burnout
escapes
giving away our power and identity
discouragement
quick fixes
procrastination
disrespecting self
shifting responsibility
blaming
putting off spiritual growth
projecting our parents' character onto God
constant criticism
believing lies
stagnation and being stuck
being the victim
blocking out love
emptiness

We welcome

the fullness of love, everlasting and overflowing
the recovery of a clear view
connection
happiness
intimacy
understanding
exploration
remembering
joy
initiating psychological and spiritual growth
our eternal nature and eternal purpose
self-respect
meaning

wisdom

creativity and movement

eternal worth

beauty

gentleness

reliability and consistency

compassion

listening

bliss

success

a larger understanding of God

Freedom and growth can begin to occur when you have the courage to let go. Letting go, even if we are letting go of something we don't want, still feels like a loss. For those of you who have experienced a lot of losses in your lifetime, it is understandable that you do not look forward to another apparent "loss." For this reason, it is important that you learn how to create safety within yourself so that you can engage in this process of letting go. Teach yourself by your actions that you are able to take care of yourself. Start being loving to yourself and you will feel safe. You have the ability as an adult to make your own choices. Choose to open your hands, relax your grasp, release the "bad" you have taken in and internalized, walk away from any destructive patterns that have been passed down to you, and walk toward love. Choose to create a more loving and meaningful life for yourself.

## Learning How to Let Go

Let's explore what this process looks like.

Imagine a young girl, Sarah, growing up in a military family that moves from place to place. Her father is very strict and is gone for long stretches at a time. Her mom is relatively good-natured yet quite busy and somewhat resentful that she is left with all the duties of raising her two kids and keeping the house running smoothly. Because there is such a lack of a stable environment combined with a lack of consistent love, Sarah develops an inordinate desire for stability. "Stability at any cost" is the life motto she develops. At fifteen she argues with her mom for hours because her mother wants to give away her old clothes and old furniture. Her mom insists that she at least get rid of something: "Sarah, we move so often, you cannot drag around that much!" Sarah insists on keeping everything. It becomes a strain for Sarah to let go of anything she has acquired. She also doesn't really want anything new. The thought of moving once again to a new home or leaving her home to go to college is almost unbearable.

In wanting to offer ourselves stability, many of us lose our balance and objectivity. We become confused when discerning what to let go of and what to hold on to, when to let go and when to hold on. Some of us respond in the extreme by holding tightly to all things, while others of us have a tendency to throw things out before they are in our hands for more than a day. King Solomon, in his wisdom, confirmed that there is a time for everything.

> A time for every purpose under heaven: . . .
> A time to mourn,
>   And a time to dance;
> A time to cast away stones,
>   And a time to gather stones;
> A time to embrace,
>   And a time to refrain from embracing;
> A time to gain,
>   And a time to lose;
> A time to keep,
>   And a time to throw away.
>
> Ecclesiastes 3:1, 4-6

What happens to Sarah as she continues to grow is what happens to each of us when our desires become inordinate and undirected. She wants more than anything else to provide herself with consistency and stability. She experienced so much chaos in her childhood that she wants to maintain as much regularity as she can. In college she begins to date men who mistreat her, neglect her, or try to control her. She wants to escape from the relationships she forms, yet she longs for consistency more than she desires her own physical protection. She thinks she is providing stability for herself because at least she knows that if she does what her boyfriend says, or walks on eggshells for him, she won't have to deal with the possible pain of losing him. In addition to this, she is familiar with a quite controlling father. Her boyfriends relate to her in a similar way. *Even if it is cruel*, she reasons, *at least it is predictable*.

This is what happens to you when your ideas of what things to let go of and when to let them go are disordered. You hold on tightly to things that take up all of the room in your heart, mind, and psyche (soul). In so doing, you do not leave room for that which is good and truly loving. When you continue to feel empty inside, in pain, you begin to wonder what is going wrong. Instead of letting go and exploring new possibilities for love to enter, you go back to what you know and think, *I just need a little bit more of this*.

We adopt schemas and frames of mind that are similar to those of our parents, unless we are taught otherwise and develop different habits.

Tolstoy emphasizes:

> To tell the truth is the same as to be a good tailor, or to be a good farmer, or to write beautifully. To be good at any activity requires practice: no matter how hard you try, you cannot do naturally what you have not done repeatedly.[1]

If you have repeatedly followed some of your old patterns of self-destruction, you do those naturally. It is quite "unnatural" for you to begin letting go of them now, after so many years, and replacing them with loving actions and behaviors.

We saw above how even though Sarah wanted something different from that which her parents gave her, she was unwilling to let go because she was afraid that the unknown and the new would be more painful than the familiar, difficult patterns. She was rigid in her thinking about instability. She thought,

*More than anything else I do not want instability.* Our pain often blinds us to the eternal truth underneath our pain and keeps us from achieving harmony. If Sarah could give herself the courage or trust God for the courage to look beyond her pain and her fear of instability, she would see that *real love brings about stability.*

Like Sarah we hold on to our old stuff for particular reasons. We took them as truth because some part of us thought they were true. We were unwilling to let them go because we thought they would bring us happiness. When we continued to find misery, we just thought that we had to deal with the misery better—and hope that love would come along. You cannot get stability if you place stability before love. When you put love before stability, you get both love *and* stability.

Sarah thought that she was giving herself love (her initial idea of love, which was the opposite of chaos), but what she was really giving herself was a life where her boyfriends controlled her actions and she continually felt unloved and unappreciated. She had not been taught, had not learned, or just had not embraced the idea that to pursue eternal love was what would ultimately bring her stability and happiness. This love includes treating yourself with respect and protecting yourself from abusive situations.

The writings of Aristotle, more than two thousand years old, tell us many of the same things that psychology books do today. He warns us of the very same danger of forming dysfunctional habits in early childhood: "It makes *no small difference,* then, whether we form habits of one kind or another from our very youth; it makes a very great difference, or rather *all* the difference."[2]

The problem we find, as clinicians, is that many people do not want to form new habits. Letting go of the old could be painful. We see this all the time with those who begin smoking at an early age. They grow up, begin to read, and learn more about the dangers of smoking, yet it is now both an emotional habit and a chemical addiction that they do not want to let go.

Unless something happens to create an awareness within us, revealing that we are able to nurture ourselves with real love and that we *deserve* to be nurtured, we will remain in the same patterns we have engaged in for years. Though we intend to change, we often return to the patterns that have been ingrained in us from our youth. This is what psychologists refer to when they speak of people living on a subconscious level.

Sarah realized that she was in pain, and she thought she was offering herself stability, but she didn't realize she was repeating the patterns her parents had shown her and thus re-creating instability. Sarah's mother and father actually pursued stability their own way. They thought that they would find stability by moving to a new town every time things didn't seem to be working right in the old one. Sarah's dad thought he could create stability by being a dictator in the family and being overly strict. Both of Sarah's parents wondered why they kept finding instability and chaos. They didn't realize they were creating it because their philosophical and spiritual priorities were out of order.

Once we have awakened an awareness and a desire to nurture ourselves and provide opportunities to create unbreakable bonds, we can proceed to the actual fun of forming them. To form these bonds we engage in a process of letting go of our old patterns and habits, which block us from intimacy, and replacing them with skills and eternal wisdom, which lead us toward connection. It is important in this process that we actively seek out teaching, training, wisdom, and understanding of ourselves and the world around us and try to apply what we have learned.

Bonds don't form from reading one chapter or one book or from one afternoon of application. Forming intimate relationships is a process that requires listening, learning, and letting go. This is at times a painful journey, yet ultimately it will lead us to what we truly desire, to wholeness and true happiness.

## Why We Are Afraid to Let Go

I have heard of ancient monkey traps that work like this: The trappers place appealing food, like an orange, inside a small cage with horizontal bars that are close together. The monkey reaches in for the orange by sliding his hand in between the bars; he then makes a fist over the orange that he desperately wants. As long as he holds on to the fruit, he cannot slip his hand out between the bars. He sits there, not willing to let go of the orange, and the trappers are able to capture him.

The monkey gives up his freedom by refusing to let go. He does not understand that the pain of letting go, in this instance, will bring him freedom, fullness, and happiness in the long run. He is hungry for the fruit that he has in his hand, and yet his stomach stays empty, because the fruit in his hand gives him a false promise of something that in actuality is not being delivered. If he had let go, he would have been free to find trees filled with bananas and oranges. In our emotional desperation we often hold on to what we have, even if it is not feeding us. The "promise" is worth more to us than the spiritual destruction that is occurring inside.

We are beginning to see, then, the problem of letting go. In letting go there is a *loss*. Yet it is a loss of something that is usually an illusion, or it is like a drug that makes us high for an hour. Like the monkey, we think, *If I let go, I'll miss out on something really valuable.* We surely do not *want* to invite more loss into our lives. Loss means sadness, and many of us are petrified of experiencing sadness. The reality is, by holding on we are already experiencing sadness. It is just disguised in the form of anger, depression, anxiety, perfectionism, addiction, and eating disorders. We are losing our very selves. If we let go, we have nowhere to go but up.

Jesus asked a very important question: "What good will it be for a man if he gains the whole world, yet forfeits his soul?" (Matt. 16:26 NIV). If you destroy the essence of your being—the growth of love inside you and your spiritual identity—what have you truly gained that is worth more than that?

Another difficulty we find in letting go is that usually we have something tangible in our hands that we think is going to bring us pleasure and happiness. When we let go of it, we do not yet have anything tangible in our hands, yet we have opened the doors of our own freedom. This is the very essence of faith. Though we are made of both matter and spirit, we live in a very material world. Many people are seeking spiritual growth and awareness and seeing their benefits, yet the scientists are still pushing for "measurable results." We want something tangible so that we *know* we've got something good! The good that we can encounter and invite within us is not always available in a tangible form.

We do not want to invite loss and sadness, because we think that to experience sadness would immobilize us. Yet we must travel through this sadness if we want to forge a new path, create a new story, and build unbreakable bonds.

Many of my clients express their fears of letting go:

> "I feel that if I let myself cry, I won't stop crying and I will be utterly out of control."
>
> "I feel like I have a huge box that I have been sitting on for the longest time. If I open it, who knows what will come out!"
>
> "I just don't want any more sadness in my life."
>
> "I don't know what is out there. How can I let go and open myself up to so many possibilities?"
>
> "I feel like I am walking toward death, but I know I am walking toward love."

I know the freedom and joy that await my clients if they choose to let go of their misery, but I cannot force them to change. I can't tell them it will all be immediately beautiful after they let go of what keeps them bound—their parents' criticism, their alcohol, their early formed patterns of self-neglect. Their lives will be more real, no doubt, and joy will be within their reach, yet there will be pain as they let go.

Fantasy writer and Scottish pastor of the 1800s George MacDonald describes the essence of the peace found in letting go:

> You will not sleep, if you lie there a thousand years, until you have opened your hand and yielded that which is not yours to give or to withhold. . . . You may think you are dead, but it will

be only a dream; you may think you have come awake, but it will still be only a dream. Open your hand, and you will sleep indeed—then wake indeed.[3]

This process takes much courage. It takes courage for each of us to let go of the patterns that are so entrenched in us but that cause us misery. We commend those of you who are on this path. We are proud of you.

## Creating the Safety to Free Yourself

When we cause ourselves pain and misery, we are usually making the best choice we can *from the model of choices we have been given.* In therapy we often see the consequences for children who come from emotionally malnourished families, just as a physician can tangibly see the consequences for those children coming from physically malnourished circumstances. When we become adults, we can choose to nourish our minds and souls. Here is a therapeutic plan that each of us can individualize according to the areas in which we are undernourished and the places that have been neglected.

1. *Guard your heart* by giving it love. No one is saying you need to throw down all your defenses and let anyone you see come barging right in. The Book of Proverbs (where we seek out wisdom) tells us it is important to guard our hearts: "Above all else, guard your heart, for it is the wellspring of life" (Prov. 4:23 NIV). Many of us think we are guarding our heart when we live subconsciously, according to our fear, holding on to the hope that our parents or someone else will show up and care for us. If we are depending on everyone else to guard our heart, then we feel insecure because we do not know when or if they will show up. When we actively choose to guard our heart from unsafe people and from destructive patterns within ourselves, our heart feels safe, and love is free to fill its rooms. We can choose to give ourselves freedom and take care of ourselves. To truly guard our heart is to guard our mind, emotions, and will.

These next steps are truly crucial for creating the safety to let go and ultimately for preparing your heart for love.

2. *Be honest* with yourself and others in all that you say. This is how we become confident that we can be counted on and that we are reliable and consistent.

3. *Focus on the goal you see* and on what you determine is most important for you. By focusing your eyes straight ahead and determining your direction, you will be less distracted or tempted to leave your new course for old destructive habits.

4. *Be proactive.* Do what it takes to create a level path before you. Think about your actions and their consequences. Embrace love and initiate ways to invite love into your thoughts and actions. Keep your feet from paths that distort the good, that promise immediate pleasure but end up stealing from your health, soul, and happiness.

Courageously guard your heart, mind, and will by connecting with and directing what you say, see, and do.

5. As before, *invite wisdom* to join you in guarding your heart.

> My son, give attention to my words;
> Incline your ear to my sayings.
> Do not let them depart from your eyes;
> Keep them in the midst of your heart;
> For they are life to those who find them,
> And health to all their flesh.
>
> Proverbs 4:20–22

We can have all the passion, emotion, and desires in the world, yet if we do not have wisdom to guide our feelings, we become a jumble of piano keys, high notes and low notes, all playing with no pattern, no melody, no rhythm, and no harmony with the other notes within us or with the notes of the others who surround us. Without wisdom, and without the mind, we do not create our own unique song.

6. *Get understanding.* Understand what has led you to this place. Understand why you stay here, what you get from re-

maining stuck where you are, unwilling to let go. Understand what triggers you are most susceptible to that lead you back to this same place: What is your state of mind?

Do you seek out what is true? Do you learn to make available to yourself more choices than your parents gave you? What is your emotional state? To whom are you connected? Are you anxious, worried, depressed, and angry?

What is your physical state? Are you well rested, exercising, eating well?

Have you been working too hard, not taking breaks, vacations, or recovery time? What is your spiritual state? Do you take time for daily prayer and meditation? Do you feel distant and dry spiritually?

7. *Invite courage.* This step is one of the most important. The secret to letting go is actually doing it! You show what you want by what you do. What we all need in order to be able and willing to say good-bye to the blockades to intimacy is courage. This doesn't mean we just wait for courage to show up. When we look up the word *courage,* we find: "mental or moral strength to venture, persevere, and withstand danger, fear, or difficulty; implies firmness of mind and will in the face of danger or extreme difficulty." To be courageous does not mean we are without fear. Courage is found in facing our fears and persevering until we reach our goal.

Where in the world do we get this courage? This is true, inner courage we are talking about, not reckless abandonment of self. As the client previously mentioned said, "I feel like I am walking toward death, but I know I am walking toward love." There *must be* a certain death of oneself so that new life can emerge. This is the exact opposite of suicide. Suicide is giving in to fear and thinking death is the only out. Courage is letting go of fear, even the fear of death itself, for we often think we are going to die if we offer ourselves something our parents did not offer us. It is letting go of the orange, freeing ourselves to trust that we can show up for ourselves. This courage is walking toward life, real life, life with love in our hearts. In this embracing of love and wholeness we are resolved to face whatever is in front of us and whatever loss may occur because we have an informed faith and understanding that we are actually providing ourselves with more in the long run.

A mother, if she sees her child in danger, will run to protect him or her. There are records of women lifting up cars that have rolled over on their husband or on one of their children. They instinctively and courageously do whatever it takes to protect the ones they love.

There is a verse that reminds us to encourage one another toward love and good deeds (Heb. 10:24). Begin to invite courage into your life. This is accomplished by creating stability within yourself, by getting to know a consistent God who loves, by being trustworthy and keeping your word, by not stealing love from others or yourself, by not giving in to your fear, by recognizing what was malnourished in childhood and teaching yourself or learning from someone how to truly nourish.

We invite courage also by surrounding ourselves with courageous friends. Choose to surround yourself with people who want to engage in life, who not only want to seek the best for themselves but do so daily. It is true that we tend to become like those around us. We have an opportunity to begin to surround ourselves with people who also pursue love and wholeness, people who are encouraging and actually want to connect—who *do* connect! As we learn to apply these principles in our own lives, we will be attracted to others who do so as well, and they will be attracted to us!

## The Power of Love

We have heard that love is powerful and can conquer all things. We know that Jesus said if we have faith the size of a mustard seed we can move mountains. God does not want to withhold this love from us, yet so often we are afraid to take it. Jesus also said if we leave home or mother or father or anything for his sake, we will gain more in this world and in the world to come. If Jesus is God, and God is Love, and God created all that is of love, what do we think we are losing when we let go of all that impedes us from connecting to love?

When we open our eyes to the possibilities God has in store for us, we see that all things are possible. In 1 John 4:18 we read, "Perfect love casts out fear." When we let go of fear, we open our hearts to love. If you do not yet know this love within your heart, know that it is within your reach. Discover your purpose; discover what it is to invite love to live within you, to become whole, and to share this love with others.

Move mountains with your faith. Let nothing stop you. Be effective. Love cannot be defeated. Learn from love. Say good-bye to fear and learn how to draw from love and fill yourself with the encouragement you find. Love yourself where you are, as you are, and encourage yourself to invite more love into your heart.

The baby bird will never fly unless it leaves the nest. You don't have to force yourself out. Give yourself the opportunity that is right in front of you—fly. Let nothing from your past crush you any longer. Let go of fear so that you can open your heart and prepare it for limitless love.

Read the following poem and consider what it means for your life.

### Anyway

People are unreasonable, illogical, and self-centered.
LOVE THEM ANYWAY
If you do good, people will accuse you of selfish ulterior motives.
DO GOOD ANYWAY
If you are successful, you win false and true enemies.
SUCCEED ANYWAY
The good you do will be forgotten tomorrow.
DO GOOD ANYWAY
Honesty and frankness make you vulnerable.
BE HONEST AND FRANK ANYWAY
What you spend years building may be destroyed overnight.
BUILD ANYWAY
People really need help but may attack you if you help them.
HELP PEOPLE ANYWAY

Give the world the best you have and you'll get kicked in the
  teeth.
  GIVE THE WORLD THE BEST YOU'VE GOT ANYWAY

> From a sign on the wall of Shishu Bhavan,
> the children's home in Calcutta
> where Mother Teresa worked[4]

# nine

# Practicing the Art of Love

Just slap on anything when you see a blank canvas staring at you like some imbecile. You don't know how paralysing that is, that stare of a blank canvas, which says to the painter: you can't do a thing. That canvas has an idiotic stare that mesmerises some painters so much that they turn to idiots themselves. Many painters are afraid in front of the blank canvas, but the blank canvas is afraid of the real, passionate painter who dares and who has broken the spell of "you can't" once for all.

Life itself, too, is forever turning an infinitely vacant disheartening, dispiriting blank side towards man on which nothing appears, any more than it does on a blank canvas. But no matter how vacant and vain, how dead life may appear to be, the man of faith, of energy, of warmth, who knows something, will not be put off so easily. He wades in and does something and stays with it.

Vincent van Gogh

You have prepared for yourself a blank canvas. As the new day brings a new sunrise and a new morning, so also there is a new land with new opportunities presented to you. As you let go of your old perceptions, your long-held bitterness, and your hope that your parents will come along to fill you with what you still lack, you enter on a new creation, a beautiful opportunity for nurturing and love to finally occur. Imagine van Gogh, staring at his blank canvas, feeling paralyzed, wondering what he will create.

Imagine a museum, such as the Louvre in Paris. All of the amazing paintings began at the same place—a blank canvas. Every home, every building, every structure you see in the world around us began with an architect staring at a blank sheet of draft paper. It is incredible to consider what the human mind can create. The same opportunity is yours today. Nothing is stopping you. The core of your person, your very soul, wants to be loved and connected. You want to be alive with vibrant color, with a design, aligned with your purpose for being here on this earth. You are able; you have already begun the process. This chapter is about committing to the process of responding to the love that is available to you on a daily basis. You get to see what it looks like to form a meaningful and connected life, to create a new painting each day, which becomes the whole painting of yourself. You can choose not to let the blank canvas intimidate you but recognize that you have all the love in the world and you have a limitless imagination. Truly you can create whatever kind of life you want to create for yourself. By wisdom you get to practice the truth that you discover and bring love into your daily life.

## Setting Up Your Canvas of Limitless Possibilities

Your focus is steady, fixed on the canvas of your life. As you connect within yourself, practicing the skill of listening to your inner expressions, you give yourself room to be alive and continue to connect with your eternal reason for being here. As a child you waited to see which paints you would have access to. You were given the lines between which you could create. You were told the worth of your painting before it was even created.

Now you are in control; you hold the brush; you create the landscape in which to live. You teach yourself the truth of your value, your worth. You invite love eternal to teach you. You take the darkness that was once in your life and use it, inviting grace to transform it to accent the light in your new painting.

Whatever your past pain has been, it has changed you. You are a deeper person because of it. In response to your pain, you searched for meaning and made efforts to find order, to find the picture of yourself, hidden deep within you, which was longing to be drawn. You have already traveled on the roads where you perpetuated your pain, recreating the painting of childhood. Now you see before you that there is a different road, a small road you hardly noticed before. Although this path is less traveled than the one you were on, you will take it and you will stay your course. You will break the spell of "I can't" once and for all.

For each of us, to let go of the old and step into the new land of creating new patterns and habits is truly like walking onto a blank canvas or discovering the moon! As a psychologist and a psychiatrist, we do not tell each individual client what his or her landscape will look like, only that we will be with them in this part of their process of discovery. They no longer have to be children. They can be adults and are able to take care of themselves no matter where they go. They also connect with their longings, purpose, and deeper self. They learn to direct themselves on their chosen path, creating silence daily in their lives, to remember to let go of the things that hold them back. They have built a trust with themselves so that they *can* walk forward into the unknown. In their engagement with their own growth in the therapeutic process, they have given themselves the opportunity to be honest with themselves, revealing and acknowledging their inner secrets. They have both set themselves free and been set free by the grace of a loving God who wants no one to be enslaved. Their bitterness has been released and their expectations let go. Their dreams are in front of them as they take the opportunity to live in freedom.

This area of the psyche is literally *unknown* to many. Who dares to paint as van Gogh did, and continue, as he did, even when none of his paintings were sold? Who dares to dedicate himself or herself to training for travel to the moon or becoming an Olympic athlete or being the person he or she was created to be? You have this incredible opportunity in front of you each day of your life! None of us knows how long this life of ours is, yet we have right now, this very moment, to embrace. You have this day before you, the day you are living in. No matter what happens, this is *your* life, and by the providence of God you will be here to live it!

If you think that your new commitment to connecting is like an exploration in space, you will be excited by the new things you discover. You can teach yourself how to respond with courage instead of fear and running away. You can learn how to be patient and gentle with yourself instead of harsh and critical, knowing that this new experience is awkward for all of us. In your gentleness toward yourself, in this awkward place, you learn to be more gentle and loving toward others. As you continue on, you become less afraid of the differences of others. You open your mind to new experiences. You do not know what to expect, but you know how to take care of yourself and trust God with each step of this new experience. You grow into a new understanding and experience of who God really is. You begin to experience God in a personal and spontaneous way rather than predictably and by rote.

## Responding to Love: The Challenge

So here is the challenge. How do you, like van Gogh, take the blank canvas called "today" and begin to paint a new life for yourself that is filled with the colors of love? How can you wake up each day and choose to make your life more colorful, as well as the lives of those around you whom you touch with your own gifts of love?

I'd like to share a personal story of how I (Paul) made some midlife adjustments in my connecting and responding to love habits. On November 15, 1989, at age forty-four, I was driving home from work, listening to the Psalms on cassette tape. I heard a strange verse in Psalm 66 talking about men flying over my head and God delivering me from fire and water. I made a left turn at about forty miles per hour at a large intersection right into the path of an oncoming car going about fifty miles per hour. We collided head-on, and my car flew way up into the air and flipped totally around, end over end.

As my car flipped, I surprised myself, because I was at total peace. My mind thought, *Oh, this is what God has in store for me today.* My car landed upside down on its roof, smashed like an accordion everywhere except where I sat. Steam and hot water spewed out of the radiator, and I thought the car could explode very soon, so I unhooked my seat belt while hanging upside down, broke my window with my elbow, and crawled out.

I ran over to the lady who had run into me. Neither of us had a scratch, even though both cars were totaled. Then I stupidly climbed back into my car to get my cassette tape and my *Dallas Cowboy Weekly*. As a policeman pulled up, the ambulance was leaving, empty.

"Where's the body?" the cop asked me.

"I am the body," I replied. He was shocked that no one died in my car.

A lady who had witnessed the accident recognized me from some of my TV appearances and gave me a ride home. That night I woke up with an intense "God dream." I've had about a dozen of them in my life, since I've been praying and meditating on Scripture daily since age ten.

Jesus was in this dream, telling me to "get that cassette tape and listen to it until I show you a verse that hits you between the eyes." I was shaken. I jumped out of bed, found the tape, stuck it into a tape player, and listened to it until a verse literally floored me. It was Psalm 90:12, "Teach us to number our days, that we may walk wisely on the earth."

There it was! God was telling me to pretend that I had died on November 15, 1989, and to consider *every single day* from then on a gift to be my own van Gogh in order to paint opportunities to love and be loved and serve God, one day at a time.

155

I called my godly mother-in-law to tell her about the car accident and my dream, and she told me something that stunned me even more. Three days earlier she had been reading Psalm 90:12, then fell asleep and had a bad dream about one of her kids having a car accident. She had been praying daily that God would protect her kids and their mates.

After that, I decided to invest *less* time seeing patients and *more* time forming unbreakable bonds with family and friends. I didn't have a prayer partner at the time, and God brought an old friend, Dave Larson, to my mind.

Dave and I were psychiatry residents together at Duke University Medical School in the 1970s. We were in the same Bible study back then and both personally trained by a brilliant Christian psychiatrist, Dr. Bill Wilson.

Dave eventually went into full-time research on spirituality to fulfill his dream—to help scientists accept Christianity and the power of connecting to God. My dream was to help Christians accept true science and psychiatric help for mental illness and to help them become more open and whole, and less legalistic, in their relationship with God. That's because I grew up in a legalistic church where I got spanked for using scissors on the Sabbath and couldn't play cards, go to movies, or dance. Jesus would have been kicked out of our church for having long hair and turning water to wine as his first miracle.

Dr. Dave Larson and I were both dreamers and both wanted to change the world. We served together for one week every six months on Focus on the Family's Physician's Resource Council. After my car accident in 1989, we called each other on the phone every couple of weeks, confessed our sins to each other, prayed for each other, and encouraged each other through our individual trials and tribulations.

One week before I wrote this chapter, Dave was exercising with his personal trainer and had a heart attack and died at age fifty-four. At the time of his death, 60 percent of the medical schools in the United States were already teaching future doctors courses on spirituality that Dr. Larson created. He and his wife, Susan, had written scores of research articles on the total health benefits of connecting with God and with others and of church attendance.

When Dave and I were in medical school in the seventies, we weren't allowed to even mention God. The ultraliberals of the day were in control. I was caught praying with a patient once and told I'd be kicked out if I ever did it again. Twenty-five percent of Freudian psychiatrists didn't even consider their treatment of a patient complete if the patient still believed in the existence of God, whom Freud considered a "rubber crutch."

In December 2001 nearly half of the psychiatrists in the United States read a thirty-six-page article on spirituality by Dave and Susan Larson and took a quiz on it. This was for continuing medical education credits. They had to read an article on the importance of prayer and spirituality to keep their medical license! What a difference between 1976 and 2002! Scientists now, for the most part, are more open to spiritual possibilities. In 1976 scientists were just as "religious" about their atheism and as intolerant as the ultralegalistic religious leaders I grew up with. And in 2002 the vast majority of Christians have left the Dark Ages. Now they confess to each other and get good psychological help if they need it. After all, whom did Jesus preach against the most when he had his public ministry two thousand years ago? It was the legalistic religious leaders of his day, the scribes and Pharisees, whom he called (to their faces) "a generation of snakes and vipers."

See what bonding can do? Neither Dave nor I would have moved religion and science even a millimeter without the prayers and encouragement we gave each other during the many times we both felt like giving up.

I called Dave the week before he died. (By the way, he had no knowledge of any heart trouble.) I wept for joy with Dave on the phone because I was so proud to be his friend, and I thanked him for the inspiration he had been to me and to the world for the past twenty-seven years. He thanked me for the same things as we reminisced about our past together at Duke up to our present together in 2002.

Why did we do that? I think God inspired us to say good-bye to each other without even knowing we were doing so. I miss

Dave and look forward to joining him in heaven someday. I would have gladly died in Dave's place.

Other things that I have changed since my car accident include spending a lot more time having fun with other married couples, mostly from our church. Because of my legalistic past, I especially enjoy taking part in our bridge club, playing Pinochle with our closest friends, going to movies, and enjoying the things my church considered sins thirty years ago.

And I've become better at "processing" with my wife, my kids, my friends, and even my employees. I encourage these people to confront me by "speaking the truth in love" and to analyze me as I practice the art of loving and being loved.

I make mistakes. Sometimes I say things or do things that offend these loved ones. When they confront me without rejecting me, it helps me see the subtle things I do that accidentally alienate or distance others.

If I start to get in an argument with my wife, we both stop and try to "step outside ourselves" and analyze what is really happening. We may agree to disagree or we may make changes, but either way, we feel closer than we did even before the argument. We have learned much more about each other and our desires.

What really helps us learn to improve our ability to love and be loved by others and ourselves is (1) truth, (2) grace, (3) love, over enough (4) time. I learned this from my colleagues, Dr. John Townsend and Dr. Henry Cloud, with whom I do live radio (along with Steve Arterburn) to an audience of about two million people each week.

By *processing* as a continual habit with all our loved ones, we learn and teach the truth to each other. What *processing* means to me is simply to step back and think about the choices that I make or made and consider: *Where did that action or choice come from? Was that the most loving choice I could have made? Did that choice reflect the highest order of priorities, "real love," not my idea of love, based on what will make me happy in the immediate?* And also, *What was I really wanting from the other person I was relating to? How can I begin to provide that for myself, instead of feeling like a victim and/or empty if he or she does not provide it for me?* I can also sit with my wife or a close friend and process with them. In doing this, I am mostly listening. I am not invested in changing the other person. I am invested in working with him or her to see what was disordered, what was not in accordance with love, and why the person chose that or was thinking about making a destructive choice.

We can experience the grace of unconditional love from each other in spite of our faults. We feel each other's love, which increases our ability to finally love ourselves in a biblically healthy way. The longer we do this, the easier it gets. Truth, grace, and love over time—this is a wonderful, biblical formula.

Since November 15, 1989, my friendship with God has improved. Ever since my upside-down car accident that day, I have prayed for four things each day.

1. Jesus, help me to become more like you—to love and be loved the way you do it. Romans 8:29 says that God knew us before we were even born and chose for me to change my character so it would be less and less like Paul Meier's "original" and more and more like Jesus. He still wants me to be myself, but with more love in my heart, like Jesus, who died on the cross to pay for all your sins and mine.

2. Jesus, help me to serve you today. Help me to help others today because helping others is so exciting and fun I can hardly stand it. Matthew 6:33 tells us *not* to live for selfish gain, but to seek first to further God's kingdom. For instance, at the beginning of my career I chose to teach at Dallas Seminary for $12,600 a year instead of running someone's clinic for $150,000 a year, because I felt I could better serve God by preparing pastors for counseling. There weren't any textbooks on Christian psychology in 1976, so I had to write my own for each course I taught, and I've written two books a year ever since that have sold millions of copies in dozens of languages. Seek first God's kingdom. All those other things he'll add to you later.

3. Help me stay out of trouble today, Jesus. In other words, "Lead me not into temptation, but deliver me from evil." If we stay out of trouble today, we've had a pretty good

day. The apostle James said we all fail in many ways. Every day of my life I have selfish thoughts or greedy thoughts or hurtful thoughts or vengeful thoughts, and sometimes I act on them, even on purpose. That's what I loved about Dave Larson. I could confess any sin to him, and he would encourage me, rebuke me, pray for me, but still love me— just like God does. We have a God of grace. He longs for our repentance, no doubt, for repentance is simply a turning away 180 degrees from our unloving acts. He gives us grace and love along our way to remind us of the love that he longs for in our lives.

4. Lord, help me to learn and grow from whatever goes *wrong* in my life today. Being a committed Christian didn't keep Dave from dying of a heart attack last week. It didn't keep my youngest daughter from running away from home when she was fourteen years old. God promises us many tribulations if we are righteous. We need them. We need flat tires. We need financial setbacks. We need diseases. We need these "thorns in the flesh" to wake us up to the pain we are causing or the deeper truth he desires us to know. He wants to keep us from being overly self-righteous or narcissistic Christians. So I expect things to go wrong. Romans 8:28 tells me God will use all of these to help me grow. Whenever a whole day goes by and nothing goes wrong, I consider that a "bonus" day— not something I should expect. Psychiatrist Scott Peck so wisely said in *The Road Less Traveled:* "Life is difficult." (Cheryl reminds me that the servant boy in the movie *The Princess Bride* conveyed the same wise message to the princess: "Life is pain, your highness.") The sooner we accept that, the more we grow in humility (with much less rage toward God for not running the world the way *we* tell him to).

One of Cheryl's favorite quotes reflects this idea that we want less pain in our lives, and thus at times we are asking for less love from God in his sketch of us.

Over a sketch made idly to amuse a child, an artist may not take much trouble: he may be content to let it go even though it is not exactly as he meant it to be. But over the great picture of his life—the work which he Loves . . . as intensely as a man loves a woman or a mother a child—he will take endless trouble—and would, doubtless, thereby give endless trouble to the picture if it were sentient. One can imagine a sentient picture, after being rubbed and scraped and re-commenced for the tenth time, wishing that it were only a thumb-nail sketch whose making was over in a minute. In the same way, it is natural for us to wish that God had designed for us a less glorious and less arduous destiny; but then—we are wishing not for MORE Love—but for less.[1]

Four years after my life-changing accident, I had another very intense dream that my sons and I were up on a hill overlooking a California highway. Soon we saw my daughter Cheryl driving down the highway, then suddenly stopping for no reason at all, then someone crashing into her car from the back end. I saw a big cartoon ambulance come to the rescue, but Cheryl was okay, so the ambulance skipped over her car and left her there alone.

I was so shaken by the dream that I woke up and asked my wife, Jan, if we ought to call Cheryl in California to warn her to drive carefully that day. We decided not to. I didn't want Cheryl to think I was an overly paranoid father—it would have confirmed any suspicion she already had. So we prayed for her instead and called our friend Robert Wise, who also prayed for Cheryl. Later that day Cheryl was driving down a California highway near her house when her brakes locked, her car started turning out of her lane, and another car crashed into hers from behind. Fortunately, no one was hurt. The man who hit her had been rushing home to his pregnant wife who was experiencing complications.

Cheryl called us to tell us about the accident, and we told her about my dream and our prayers for her possible accident that day, much like my mother-in-law prayed for me before I had my car accident.

Why does God work this way? I think I have some under-standing of why. I think God wants to remind us that even if our earthly fathers and mothers aren't there for us, he is, even in times of trouble, sorrow, disease, or even the death of those whom we love. We need unbreakable bonds with God and oth-ers in this life to give our life joy and meaning. We must *choose,* in this difficult life, to practice the art of loving and being loved.

# ten

# Connection
# with Protection

Love is patient, love is kind. . . . it is not easily angered, it keeps
no record of wrongs. . . . It always protects.

1 Corinthians 13:4, 5, 7 NIV

Like a city that is broken into and without walls
Is a man who has no control over his spirit.

Proverbs 25:28

Bill was an angry man with a severe temper. He was a forty-
year-old rage-aholic. He came to the Paul Meier New Life day
program in Dallas only because his wife said she would leave
him if he didn't get help. Bill was a sports agent and lawyer
from Los Angeles. He had been arrested nine times for getting
into fights in various situations including from road rage.
Because he was a lawyer, he managed to stay out of jail. He also
had one recent DWI. Bill was a large, six-foot-five-inch, 275-
pound man. He was muscular, with "back off" written all over
his face.

When he walked into my (Paul's) office for the first time, I was immediately scared of him and told him so. I said, "I don't even know what you're here for, but the look in your eyes scares me." Then he told me, "I'm here to work on my bad temper, because I love my wife and I want her back. She left me and won't come back until I work on my anger problem." I promptly asked about his childhood because I wondered how he could have turned out to be such a rage-aholic. I found out that he fought a lot as a child. He said he had a hard time adjusting when he was little because his family was always moving from town to town. His dad was a workaholic and was gone much of the time. When his dad was home, he was not affectionate. He was critical but not physically abusive.

Bill's dad and mom had recently begun attending church. Bill was noticing that his dad was making rather dramatic changes in his life for the better. This encouraged Bill that he might be able to change too.

Bill's mom had been physically abused as a child by her alcoholic father, so she was passive, fearful, and not very affectionate. She was afraid of everybody.

The youngest of five rough-and-tumble athletic boys, Bill was a top member in the debate team because he loved to argue. He also excelled in sports and graduated fourth in his high school class, despite abusing drugs and alcohol.

Bill was sexually abused between the ages of eight and eleven by his uncle who lived next door during those years. Because he was never close to his father, he craved male attention. Bill's paternal uncle befriended him, and when Bill began spending more and more time next door at his uncle's house, his uncle began to make him perform sexual acts with him. Bill hated this and felt very confused but didn't think he could say no and was too embarrassed to tell his parents. He had never confided in them anyway.

Bill had never been in fights until the sexual abuse occurred. He had never deeply bonded with his parents or anyone, and then when he made his first attempt at connecting, he was used and abused. He was filled with rage and shame, which he turned inward. Internalized anger eventually turns into depression. As a result of his depression, Bill spent the rest of his life getting into fights and abusing drugs and alcohol. He remained outwardly happy-go-lucky and popular, but inside he was lonely, depressed, ashamed, and bitter.

He was an officer in a number of clubs in high school and had many superficial friends, but he never shared his private feelings with them. He felt depressed and lonely all his life in spite of an outward appearance that everyone would judge as quite the opposite.

Bill graduated from college and law school by age twenty-three and promptly married his college sweetheart. She divorced him three years later because of repeated temper outbursts and physical threats of violence, even though he never actually hit her. At age twenty-nine he married Courtney, who was affectionate, deeply religious, and a very kind woman. The fact that Bill was abused growing up naturally (or unnaturally) caused him to feel out of control and afraid of the chaos of abuse. As a result of feeling out of control, he became more controlling of his surroundings, other people, and himself. Bill felt unprotected so he rigidly worked to overprotect himself from being hurt. Bill tended to be overly controlling with Courtney, which she put up with in the first few years of their marriage. Courtney was a healthy, assertive individual. She loved Bill but did not like his controlling tactics. He yelled at her frequently and threatened her when he couldn't control her decisions. She knew something had gone wrong in his childhood that made him into an angry man but didn't know what it was. She assumed it was from growing up without love in his home but never knew about the sexual abuse by Bill's uncle. She enjoyed the good qualities in Bill. He could be fun and affectionate, and he was very intelligent.

Finally Courtney became fed up with Bill's angry outbursts. She wanted to stay married to him if he would get help, but she chose not to continue living in the same house with him because of all the emotional abuse and physical threats. She was deeply concerned for their children and wanted to protect them as well.

Separation was the best thing that could have happened to Bill. It shocked him into realizing that he could lose Courtney and his children, whom he truly loved. He realized how much he longed for the bonding that he sensed could be possible with her but that he had never experienced with anyone.

He was so distraught he became suicidal and, at one point, put a gun to his head. Instead of pulling the trigger he got on his knees and asked God into his life. This was very difficult for him to do, because, like most people, he assumed God was like the distant and unprotecting authority figures he had experienced growing up. Plus he had been bitter all his life toward God for allowing his uncle to betray him.

Bill went to a local church and talked to a pastor. The pastor had come to my day program a decade ago when he had gone through a depression. He told Bill how much it had helped him. The pastor urged Bill to do the same.

In his first few days at the day program, Bill was critical of everything he saw. Some of the other patients were scared of him because he had such a hostile look. As the staff and other patients continued to show him unconditional love and respect in spite of his hostility, he began to melt. When he heard the other patients sharing their innermost thoughts and feelings, he finally confided the horrible experience he had had with his uncle and how he had let it ruin his life. The pain of his sexual abuse had caused him to choose never again to bond intimately with anyone.

The staff encouraged Bill to confront his uncle and to tell his parents the truth about what had happened to him as a child. His parents actually flew to Dallas so he could tell them in person all the things he had felt growing up, not only about his uncle but also about his relationship with them. His parents were surprisingly understanding and apologized for not showing him more affection and kindness and for not protecting him better as a child. They were shocked to find out that Bill's uncle had sexually abused him repeatedly during those years. They knew Bill's personality had drastically taken a turn for the worse during those years and always wondered why. Bill and his parents wept together for many hours. When Bill confronted his uncle over the phone about the abuse, the uncle denied it completely.

Bill explained to Courtney all the new things he had learned at the day program. He began to share his long-hidden secrets with her. He feared that he risked losing her by being so open, yet he found this new intimacy incredibly wonderful. When Courtney found out about Bill's past, she empathized, wept, and felt a deeper love and understanding for him than she ever had before. He then shared with her what he had learned about connecting, confessing, and forgiving.

Bill realized he wanted to move to a place of forgiveness toward his uncle and leave his vengeance up to God. He understood that this process would help his depression. Bill learned from the day program what research supports, that those who connect with God and with others who know all their secrets and love them anyway enjoy their lives the most. Bill's personal goal was to move from a place of insecurity and false bravado to a place of inner courage, protection, and strength. He recognized that he was already much happier now that he had begun the process of letting go of his bitterness, shame (bitterness toward self), and fear. Even though he was feeling wonderful for the moment, Bill realized that wholeness was not instantaneous. This was to be a lifelong process. His anger would resurface in different instances and phases of his life, and he would then want to work through a process of reforgiving and reprotecting.

Three weeks later when Bill left the day program, his love and joy were evident on his face. His bitterness had turned to bonding with God, his parents, Courtney and his children, and the others he had met at the day program. He learned to feel, for the first time in his life, that he was worthy of loving and being loved. He began to enjoy his own company.

We encouraged his wife to stay separated from him for a little while longer and to date him to be sure that these dramatic changes lasted. We taught her she could give Bill her love, but she couldn't give him trust because trust has to be earned. Even though we thought Bill would do well, it seemed most reasonable for her to go slowly and to wait for his actions to prove the changes were real and lasting.

A few months later we got a letter from Bill saying that he was back with his wife and two children. He said he had never experienced as much joy in his life as he was experiencing. He used his connecting experience at the day program to start building close and honest relationships with his family and with a small group of safe men from his new church.

## Conscious Connecting

Bill had been continually acting on his anger and rage left over from childhood. He had made efforts to control his temper on many occasions, but he was never very successful. This is the case for many of us. We intend to change our ways and truly connect with those we love, yet we end up exploding in rage, withdrawing, working late at the office, or feeling frustrated and unable to change our situation. Bill had truly wanted closeness with his wife and children, but he realized his fear of facing (consciously connecting with) his core problem had kept him from moving forward.

It is in knowing and applying the truth that we become free. To consciously connect with self and others, it is important to daily commit to being conscious. We may wonder if being "conscious" is merely some psychobabble term. According to Webster, to be conscious is to know, to be aware, to have knowledge of one's own sensations and feelings, to be able to feel and think.

We discover that when we *disconnect* ourselves from the bad feelings within, we end up *disconnecting* ourselves from many other feelings as well. When we exert energy to shut down sad feelings, we often find that genuine happiness is shut off as well. We haven't yet figured out a way to make a wall that blocks only the bad feelings. Conscious connecting, while also protecting yourself, is a discipline; it is not automatic. Many people say they want to be aware of their thoughts and feelings, yet they run from both, sometimes without even knowing it.

Many of us have stored up bitterness, sadness, loss, and pain, which we would rather not feel or think about. Bill, before his visit to the day program, was continually cutting off his feelings of sadness, loss, and vulnerability by covering them and numbing them with superficial social events, alcohol, and an occasional outburst of rage. This is how Bill had learned to cope as a child. As an adult he had a choice to learn how to protect himself in ways he wasn't able to in childhood. He hadn't offered himself the choice to change, or he hadn't realized yet that he could change. Instead of learning new ways to connect with himself on a deeper level, he continued to feel helpless and cope by using his well-learned rage in desperate situations. Although he longed for closeness, he ensured that he was not going to have intimacy with anyone because his anger kept close friendships from forming. *At least I'm not going to get hurt,* he thought, yet, within, he was in great pain.

## Conscious Protection

In the rest of this chapter we will explore the hidden ways we block ourselves from the very love we long for most in our lives. When we unearth the secrets of conscious connection with protection, we will learn what it is to invite love into our lives and embrace it. Instead of trying to control or cut off our feelings and actions and control or cut off the feelings and actions of others, we will learn what it is to find the secrets hidden underneath our awareness and bring them to the light of day. In choosing this enlightenment, we open up the wondrous possibility of conscious connection with others and with ourselves.

### *Step One: Consciously Connecting with Our Anger*

One of the largest factors blocking us from intimacy is our misdirected response to anger. I am amazed by the sheer number of psychological texts and self-help books that encourage us to *control* our anger and develop "anger management skills." I (Cheryl) worked like this with my clients for a long time, feeling frustrated along with them when the "controlling tactics" didn't last. Out of a desire for a better solution, I sought to develop a different perspective on anger. Dr. Allen Surkis, one of my mentors, taught me this simple understanding of anger: Whenever a person is angry, he or she feels unprotected in some way. From this I understood that, instead of running around trying to control the anger, push it down, or manage it, the angry person must go *directly* to where he or she feels unprotected and work on learning how to find protection and also understand why he or she didn't feel like this protection was deserved before.

We feel protected when our personal, spiritual/psychological, and physical boundaries are respected. Our brains, for instance, are soft yet enclosed in a thick protective skull. God made us with skin to protect and contain everything under our skin. We still learn, by our parents' teaching, not to run out onto a busy street because our lives are worth protecting. Psychological protection is also both innate and learned. When parents are constantly screaming at us we learn that our boundary of "not wanting to be yelled at" does not matter.

If in childhood we are taught that we aren't allowed boundaries, then as we grow up we do not learn to set boundaries. When we said no before, our no was ignored. In fact, we were often told "you are bad [or, you are wrong] to say no," so we learn to doubt our reasoning ability to discern when to say no and when not to. When this happens in childhood, we often become so needy for love that we learn to disregard our own boundaries and limits in order to try to please others so they will like us.

The anger works like an explosion. We recognize the incoming threat, realize our learned disability to protect ourselves, then explode to keep people distant and protect ourselves. In doing this, however, we keep love out and destroy ourselves and are often destructive toward others. We give away our power to learn how to be truly assertive, to respect ourselves, and to live with love and integrity. We react instead of consciously choosing how we want to act.

This outlook began to open doors for clients with lifelong patterns of rage and disconnection. Even those clients who did not experience rage per se were still held captive by many other disguised forms of anger—depression, guilt, frustration, irritability, or constant criticism. It has been exciting to begin to see lasting and real change—freedom in the lives of these clients who are given the tools to consciously connect while protecting themselves.

Here is how clients frequently communicate their perspective of anger:

- I don't ever become angry!
- I express my anger by cursing at people all the time on the freeway.
- I can control my anger.
- When I get angry I count to ten.
- My pastor told me whenever I get angry to just recite verses.
- When I get angry I go for a walk.
- I don't get angry, just annoyed, frustrated, disappointed, anxious.

It is true that if we count to ten or go for a walk, we may be able to gain some objectivity and discover what is at the root of our anger, what made us feel unprotected. Scripture reading and meditation *can* guide us in what to do with our hurt, which is underneath our anger. Often, however, people become so distracted by the anger or in trying to manipulate, control, or diffuse their anger, that they never understand what is beneath their anger, the causes for it.

### What's Wrong with Anger?

Some people think it is always wrong to become angry, yet even the New Testament tells us that we can be angry without sinning. The apostle Paul wrote: "'Be angry, and do not sin': do not let the sun go down on your wrath" (Eph. 4:26). Part of the confusion many of us have is that we confuse a person's anger with his or her *response* to the anger. Often a person's *response* to anger is violence, which is destructive to the person and those around him or her. Other responses to anger are criticism, sarcasm, and other forms of aggressive attacks, either verbal or physical.

We have discovered that our pain is always an indicator that something needs to be attended to. Pain, in and of itself, is not "wrong" but can be useful to communicate to us the location of where we are still unhealed. Psychological pain is as difficult to bear as physical pain and yet has much to teach us.

Anger too is not wrong in itself but an indicator that some part of us feels *unprotected*. In other words, when we begin to feel angry, we can listen to that anger and know that we are communicating to ourselves that we somehow feel vulnerable, violated, attacked, threatened, or neglected in some capacity. It is our psyche's natural way to wake us up, to motivate us to learn how to attend to ourselves, offer lasting protection, offer nurturing, and build up inner strength by putting outer boundaries in place.

Bill would get angry when Courtney made any kind of financial decision without him. His boundaries had been severely violated in childhood by his uncle who had caused him pain. In light of his experience, Bill thought that if he didn't directly control every one of Courtney's financial decisions, he would be severely injured again. Bill had a general feeling of being unprotected, which grew as he continued on in adulthood without discovering the healing he needed. His sense of unprotectedness affected every aspect of his life. Although his meticulousness and overcontrol worked well for him at times in the courtroom, it backfired any time he perceived a threat elsewhere. His response to perceived threats was either to get in fights or to drink, destroying his life along with the lives of those his drinking affected.

We can begin to see how anger in itself is not bad—it is the indicator of vulnerability or violation. When we try to ignore our anger, we often become more depressed and angry, because we are ignoring the very indicator that is communicating to us where we are being hurt.

Controlling anger doesn't do a lot to change the underlying situation or problem. It just pushes the anger down to come out in another form. We can learn, instead, how to listen to our anger and learn where our pain is, where we feel unprotected. Then we can choose to offer ourselves protection. Instead of working really hard to control our anger, it is important for us to apply that same effort and energy toward learning how to *listen* to our anger and *direct* our responses. We distract ourselves from further self-knowledge when we explode and throw tantrums. This may diffuse our anger, but we forfeit an opportunity to learn where we are vulnerable and weak and to strengthen those areas.

### Fight, Freeze, or Flight

Instinctively we react in one of three ways to a perceived threat—fight, freeze, or flight. Yet we, as humans, also have the ability to act on our thoughts and not merely respond by instinct. When we are angry, "fight" might look like exploding rage. "Freeze" might result in our being locked in bitterness. "Flight" would be our running away, pushing our anger away, and yet watching it come back to us in some misshaped way.

Instincts protect us when a sudden danger faces us and we have to respond quickly. Even then, however, if we are trained to protect ourselves, we have a better chance of survival. The martial arts teach us how to protect ourselves from attack. We learn how to respond in strength instead of freezing and being vulnerable. In the same way, *connection with protection* is a discipline through which we train and inform our instincts with the knowledge about ourselves that we have gained.

I recently heard a commentator remarking about the poor free throw performance of a professional basketball player. The commentator said the man would practice for hours, yet he practiced with the wrong form, so it didn't help his free throw. This is what happens when we continually respond to our anger by becoming violent or by holding it in and throwing it back on ourselves through depression. We reinforce our destructive responses to anger. In order to unlearn our destructive responses, it is important to equip ourselves with constructive responses, such as exploring where we feel unprotected. All the energy we used to spend on yelling at the people trying to hurt us, we can spend learning how to be adults and protect ourselves.

One good way of directing yourself to *actively respond* to a situation instead of *reacting* to it is to verbalize your intent. Suppose you have a problem with anger and you have just been cut off on the freeway. Your typical reaction to this insult is to blare your horn or tailgate the offender for the next mile and a half. The next time this happens, try communicating aloud your intent. It might sound something like this: "I'm so mad at that guy who just cut me off that I'm going to honk my horn incessantly and tailgate him down the freeway!" When we bring a reaction to life by verbalizing it, we begin to recognize how we are choosing to spend our energy. Then we can take our power back by exploring our reaction: *I wonder why that got me so irritated?* or *What part of me feels so unprotected to cause such intense anger? One instance where I felt "cut-off" in childhood was . . .*

### Step Two: Protecting or Projecting

Another way we can learn to invite protection and love to our connections is to learn where we have "projection." We each have a tendency, unless we consciously heal and change it, to follow a pattern in life that we call the 3 Ps—pick, provoke, and project. We often subconsciously fill our lives with people just like our parents.

1. We *pick* a spouse or dating partner who is like our parents. The person already seems familiar to us from across the room. Sometimes we try to pick people who are the exact opposite of our families and find out that they have surprising similarities in behavior, just disguised in a different package. If this doesn't work . . .
2. We *provoke* people to respond to us in the same way our parents did. If our parents were critical, for instance, we find ourselves constantly seeking approval from others and asking for their criticism. We provoke them to be like that which we know, because we already know how to respond to those patterns. Sadly, we have lived so long

174

within this framework, even if we are miserable, we are still comfortable in knowing that the same misery will happen today, tomorrow, and the next day. If we picked a kind person who is not easily provoked then . . .

3. We *project* familiar family traits onto the person when he or she does the smallest thing that reminds us of our parents. For instance, even if our spouse is being thoroughly attentive, when he looks the other way because he hears a noise, our suspicions are confirmed: "See, you were ignoring me!"

   In this case we are projecting neglect onto our spouse even though he or she is not neglecting us. We are so used to being neglected, we readily assume it is happening again, even when it isn't. In projection we assume our friends are just as critical or just as flaky or just as negligent as our family was to us. Our mind amplifies and projects onto them any resemblance we find that reminds us of our parents, making it more difficult to connect with those we wish to connect with.

You can choose to consciously recognize the hidden tendencies you have to pick, provoke, and project on others. Consciously connecting with others takes effort, but when we do, we protect ourselves and others and thus feel safe enough to grow closer.

## Leftover Wounds

Some psychological research suggests that when we have an argument with our friends, spouse, or boss, 20 percent of the argument has to do with the actual argument, and 80 percent has to do with unhealed wounds left over from childhood. By this we mean 80 percent of our hurt and anger comes from our seeing this person as a continuation of our parents or other people or events from our childhood. We project our ideas on people like we project images on cloud formations. If we all looked up at the different clouds and began to express to one another what forms we saw, most of us would see very different things.

This is the concept behind projective tests, such as the Rorschach inkblot test. In the inkblot test, people describe what they see in various inkblot formations. You would be amazed by the variety of things people see. For instance, if one inkblot is in the shape of a kitten, some may say it looks like a tiger; some may say it looks like a briefcase; some may say, "It looks like a big mouth that is about to swallow me." These projections are so ingrained, we do not even realize that our perceptions are different from those of others. In daily life we recognize this when we travel to foreign countries and find it so odd that people do things differently.

When we make an effort to see people as they are, without contaminating our perception with our past bad experiences, we open possibilities of really knowing them and truly being known. I had the opportunity to observe a brilliant psychologist with his patients every Wednesday for a year. Some of his patients would call him harsh. Some would say he was the nicest man in the world. Some would say he was seductive. Some would say he was critical and rude. Others would say he was intelligent, insightful, kind, and gentle. I saw him as the same person each time, but they often saw through their past experiences with fatherlike figures.

As a psychologist I have learned to listen to what my clients say in this area because I've found that not only are they communicating to me, they are also communicating to themselves in the process.

Clients all have their own ideas of what an authority figure is like. If they see authority figures as manipulative and conniving, clients will be suspicious of me from the start. If they think that authority figures are always right and are there to be put down, clients will provoke this in their therapy. If they have disdained the authority figures in their lives and have held on to bitterness, clients will often try to provoke their psychologist to say something hurtful—or they will accuse him or her of being hurtful, so that they can be rebellious, vengeful, and bitter in therapy. In doing this, however, clients are blocking their own growth.

We talk freely about these kinds of things in therapy so that clients can choose to contribute to their own growth instead of trying to pick fights. It is important, however, to allow these thoughts and feelings to surface, because then the client realizes what he or she is doing in voicing projections. Then the person can draw closer to the core of his or her difficulties and see people with less distortion and see where he or she has been stuck or what perceptions he or she has accepted. The person begins to let go of the dysfunctional and invite the more functional, worthwhile, and clearer perceptions to develop. I have had clients who were staunch atheists before beginning therapy. After a process of letting go of their projections, they began pursuing a relationship with a God their eyes had never been opened to before. We perceive the events in life through the filter we have developed since early childhood.

### Understanding Others

When we become aware of our own ability to project our past perceptions onto other people and we become aware that others do the same thing, then we can listen more compassionately. We take things much less personally and are able to listen and consider: *How much of that statement is me, and how much is not me?* There is much less fear in interacting with others because we have learned how to better protect ourselves.

We can all make conscious efforts to see people as they really are. We can intentionally let go of pasts that contaminate our present. This does not mean we are naive, insisting that everyone is genuine, nice, and wants to connect. The more authentic we become, seeking truth, wisdom, and clarity in our lives, the more grounded and secure we will be, more able to protect ourselves from those who wish to harm us, more able to love the people we meet on our life's journey, and more able to laugh and enjoy life.

## Connection with Protection Exercises

We include these practical exercises for you to use to promote conscious connection with protection in your life.

1. When you become angry, practice communicating to yourself what you feel. Explore where you may feel unloved or unprotected. Recognize your initial response choice, then consider: *What do I give myself when I* _____? Take the time to probe what prompts your response. Find a different way to use the energy you have expended on being angry. Use it to heal!

2. Pray and meditate daily. There is much research that reveals that people who pray and meditate actually live longer. Prayer transforms the body's chemicals. Thus in silence, prayer, and meditation, we consciously connect with God and are then better able to connect with others.

3. Release your projections. You can count to ten. Take a step back from whatever is going on, hone in to why your heart feels unprotected, and take an active role in protecting yourself. If you are finding it too difficult to stop in the middle of an argument or when you are angry, keep a journal of instances like these. Explore the reasons that you felt hurt and unprotected and/or why you became angry. As the entries accumulate, go back and review them. A pattern will emerge. You will notice that you felt hurt or became angry in specific situations. It may be helpful to try phrasing these situations in relation to your childhood. Change an observation such as, "I get angry when people don't listen to me," to "I feel like my parents didn't pay attention to me when I was a child." This does *not* mean that we blame our parents. We are just recognizing where the pain started so that we can move to forgiveness, let go of waiting for our parents to change it, and begin to initiate our own healing and set new boundaries. Look at the repeating patterns you see and consider: *What underlying message do I hold on to that keeps me unprotected in this way? When am I going to let go of that message? What is keeping me from letting go now?*

# Part 4

# PERFECTION

We discover ways to change how we treat ourselves so that we can mature in our ability to love.

We explore what it means to know God and develop an unbreakable bond with him.

We consider whether or not there are any medical or genetic complications keeping us from love.

# eleven

# Changing the Way I Treat Myself

Knowledge of the self puts us on our knees, and it is very necessary for love. . . . As Saint Augustine says, "Fill yourselves first, and then only will you be able to give to others."

Mother Teresa

For we know in part . . . but when perfection comes, the imperfect disappears. When I was a child, I talked like a child, I thought like a child, I reasoned like a child. When I became a man, I put childish ways behind me. Now we see but a poor reflection as in a mirror; then we shall see face to face. Now I know in part; then I shall know fully, even as I am fully known.

1 Corinthians 13:9–12 NIV

You have journeyed far to get to this section on perfection. The verb *perfect* means "to do thoroughly or to bring to maturity." In this section you are invited to continue maturing your ability to love and discover what it is to love thoroughly. You do not give yourself this fullness by *demanding perfection* from yourself, being hard on yourself, or being a perfectionist. A perfectionist crushes freedom and remains unsatisfied until perfection occurs. If you think of Jesus, as revealed in the gospels, you do not see him worrying about getting something right. He does not ever appear to be demanding perfection from himself. He was perfect in every way, not because he forced himself to be but because he knew the love of his Father thoroughly. He chose the most loving thing to do, be, and say every opportunity he had.

You can choose to have a deep commitment and an unwavering walk toward the perfect love of God, our Father, while inviting his perfect love to fill you and satisfy you for the entire journey. In doing this, you walk toward the love that *fully knows you already,* as we are reminded in the Scripture at the beginning of the chapter. You walk toward the mature and complete version of yourself that God had in mind when he created you in your mother's womb.

In this chapter we will work with you so you can learn how to perfect or mature your ability to observe the positive and negative messages you give yourself daily. It is important to learn how to direct these messages, keeping those that encourage you to obtain your ultimate goals and eliminating the messages that sabotage your growth and maturity. We are also going to explore the rewards of committing to love. You will discover what you get from becoming thoroughly united with love. As you learn to fix your eyes on the prize ahead of you, you give yourself the opportunity to persevere on your path. You freely choose to remain committed to maturity and growth in your innermost self.

## Self-Awareness

I (Paul) would like to share with you an example from my own life that reveals how our self-talk shows up uninvited, how we can choose to let it go, and how to replace it with love.

When I began teaching pastoral counseling[1] full-time at Dallas Theological Seminary in 1976, I was thirty-one years old and still had lots of self-critical and self-condemning messages floating around in my head. My father was a strict German. Often when I made mistakes around him, he would say to me, *"Du dummkopf!"* (You dumbhead!). One day I walked into my class of seventy-five students just as the bell rang. As I rushed to the podium, I realized that I had left my lecture notes in my car. I apologized to the class and asked them to wait ten minutes for me while I went out to my car in the parking lot a block or so away to get my notes. I was very embarrassed that I made this mistake in front of students whom I so much wanted to impress.

On my way to the car I said to myself furiously, *Du dummkopf!* I even said it in German. Somewhere inside of me the kind part of me replied to the cruel part of me saying, *Hey! Welcome to the human race. You are a psychiatrist. You don't have to put up with that kind of abuse! All humans make mistakes. Why should you expect yourself to be perfect, just because your father did?* Then I asked myself another question: *Paul, if your best friend were giving this lecture today and you came along to assist him and he forgot his notes and had to go to his car to get his notes and you decided to go walk with him, would you yell at him,* Du dummkopf!? I immediately replied, *Of course not!* Then I asked myself: *If you would never do this to your best friend, why do you do this to yourself?*

By now I had gotten to my car and I noticed a tree stump nearby. I stopped to say a quick prayer, "Dear God, thank you that I am not that tree stump. That tree stump can't love or be loved or experience eternity with you. It can just sit there. Thank you, God, that I am a normal human being who makes many mistakes, like other human beings."

As soon as I finished that prayer, I felt so good about myself and so at peace that I turned around and left my notes in the car again, but this time on purpose. I walked into the class and explained to the class that I decided to give a different lecture than I had planned. I wanted to teach them about the various parts of ourselves that argue with other parts of ourselves. I described to them the process I had just walked through and the choice I had just made to become my own best friend and to never again call myself a *dummkopf*. My lecture for the next ninety minutes was totally spontaneous and probably the best lecture I ever gave them. I spoke honestly with no notes except for those on my heart with which I had just connected. I encouraged all of them to write that date down in their Bibles if they wanted to make a pledge to God as I had to become their own best friend and to pay close attention to their own self-talk.

Among my earliest students were John Townsend and Henry Cloud, who are both psychologists now and do a national daily radio program with me. They are the authors of the *Boundaries* books.[2] Another student of mine was Tony Evans, who later became a doctor of theology and one of the leading African American pastors in America. If I had continued in my negative self-messages, I know I would not have been nearly as effective in teaching these men the principles from my heart that could change their lives and the lives of those to whom they minister. I would have been teaching them only facts from my head. Plus I surely would have become burned-out from beating myself up all of the time.

We are beginning to see why self-knowledge, as described in Mother Teresa's words at the beginning of this chapter, is a vital key to growth and maturity. If you just let these voices run free in your head, you let others lead you—and their destination may not be the same as yours. You have already begun to know yourself on a level you may never have thought possible before. Remember that true connection with and knowledge of yourself does not make you more self-absorbed but more humble. As Mother Teresa concluded: "Knowledge of God produces love, and knowledge of the self produces humility."[3] When we start to feel the deep love of God, we are softened by the tenderness he shows in loving us. We long to share this love with others so no one goes without his love. Often the people who become the most self-absorbed are those who have learned to disconnect from themselves and from the love of God. As you train your ability to connect with this love and give this love to yourself, you naturally want to share it with others. It is when you feel empty and disconnected that you awaken your tendency to be stingy with any love that comes your way. If I had kept calling myself a *dummkopf,* I actually would have become more and more self-absorbed in my own pain. I would have spent much of my time and energy paying closer and closer attention to everything I said so I could beat myself up at the slightest mistake. In doing this, I keep love and grace from myself and have less to give to others.

## Thorough Commitment to Love

We invite you to choose to thoroughly *commit* to the process of knowing and loving yourself in order to direct yourself toward love and free yourself to know and love others. To commit to yourself is to put yourself in charge or trust yourself. It comes from the Latin word *committere,* which means "to connect or entrust." We can choose to let go of our fear of commitment by teaching ourselves to connect with and trust ourselves. Teach yourself that you are trustworthy by *being* trustworthy with your speech and actions. To do this, it is important to let go of the word *try.* For example, "I am *trying* to know myself." The word *try* implies that you have one foot in and one foot out. Instead of *try,* use *do* or *do not.* Watch the results. You are worth a *complete* commitment. Show yourself by your actions that you are worth this much by committing to the process of knowing yourself, being kind to yourself, and directing yourself toward love.

## Unifying the "Team Members" in Our Heart and Mind

We learned in the first chapter that we all long to be known and deeply loved. We long for this, yet we have kept ourselves from this in the past. In the process of working through this book, you have been consciously recognizing and letting go of the ways you had learned to reject, disconnect, or run away from knowing your innermost self. You *wanted* love to reside in your heart, but the places where your parents or close others in your childhood failed to introduce it are the same places where you tend, as an adult, to keep it out. So also the ways that your parents or friends did not take the time to get to *know* you in childhood are often the same ways you probably have chosen not to get to know yourself.

Unless you *consciously recover the truth* that you *are* made to be known and loved, you assume from your childhood experience that you are not worth knowing. Even though I (Paul) know my father loved me, he also saw me as a *dummkopf* who made way too many mistakes to satisfy his expectations.

When I took piano lessons as a child, for example, he sat beside me with a wooden paddle and swatted me whenever I made a mistake. As a result, I hated piano lessons even though I loved music. To this day I hate to open a music book and play a song on the piano the way it is written. This is why I learned to play by ear; it was my way of rebelling against my father while reclaiming my love for music. I can hear a song for the first time on the radio and sit down and play it, but if you put the music for that same song in front of me, I won't be able to play it. Some parts of me are still being healed!

In adulthood you have the opportunity to grow into a *new* understanding of the world and how people relate. Every day you get a new opportunity to teach yourself a new model by being loving to yourself. Since I have chosen to be nice to myself, I don't let others call me a *dummkopf*. If I had continued inwardly to call myself a *dummkopf* and other names, then I would have eventually called my students and my children *dummkopfs*. I would have sought out critical friends who would have reinforced my *dummkopf* messages.

In the New Testament, Jesus reminded us, "If a house is divided against itself, that house cannot stand" (Mark 3:25). Imagine a football team where each of the players runs in any direction he chooses on every play. The players do not recognize that they have a coach, they hardly listen to him if he tries to talk, and he doesn't mind if they ignore him (he does not want to appear to be demanding). "Twenty-four, thirty-seven, hut! hut!" The football is thrown and there is chaos on the field.

The quarterback is injured because he wasn't protected by the men on the team who were meant to protect him. The ball has not moved forward. In fact it was fumbled and is now in the hands of the opposing team.

By choosing not to be united, this team chose chaos, conflict, crisis, and distrust among its members. On a football team each member has a specific job to do. If all the individual jobs are done to the best of each member's ability, they give themselves the opportunity to move the ball forward to the goal as a unified team. If the quarterback *knows*, by the repeated commitment and actual play of the offensive linemen, that they will protect him, he does not worry about being hurt or fear that he will be left vulnerable. He is free to do his job to throw the ball in the direction that he, his coach, and the whole team planned out beforehand.

It takes each member of the team to be unified, present, and committed to the process for the team to achieve the common goal. In this way, no member is more important or less important than the others. Super Bowls may be won by one kicker making a field goal. However, if the linemen had not protected the space he needed to get to the ball and kick it, it would not have happened. If the center who snapped the ball to him did not know what he was doing, the kicker would not have had the opportunity to do his job well. If the guy who catches the ball and places it into position for the kicker had not caught it and executed his job to the best of his ability, there would not have been a chance to make the goal.

So how does this relate to Jesus' statement about a house divided against itself and how does this relate to us psychologically and spiritually? When you choose to unite yourself with love, you give yourself the opportunity to get to the goal. When you do not, you create chaos, conflict, crisis, and inner insecurity. You fumble the ball of your own life to the opposing team.

This football team analogy can give you insight when you consider the members of your team.

1. Who is the coach in your brain?
2. What kind of person is he or she?

3. How do the team members relate to one another?
4. What kind of atmosphere is inside your mind?

We each hold within us conflicting desires, values, feelings, self-messages, insecurities, strengths, and ways of relating. If you choose to take a drug, you are acting on many desires at the same time; one is your desire for self-destruction and another is your desire for an immediate high, pleasure, or escape. If, at the same time, you have the desire to read a book and a desire to go for a walk, you make a choice, consciously, subconsciously, or somewhere between the two. You give the desires within yourself an order or priority based on many things, mainly:

1. what kind of person you *wish* to be
2. what kind of person you and others *think* you are
3. what kind of person you are *in actuality*

In 1976 I (Paul) wished to be a perfect person who could finally please my father. Other people thought I was smart and happy, but in actuality I was very insecure and constantly angry at myself for not being good enough to please my dad. But that moment in the parking lot, I became a person who just wished to love and be loved and to feel free to make mistakes like any other human. I connected with the part of me inside who was appreciative that he wasn't a helpless tree stump.

Your idea (or goal) of the kind of person you *wish* to be influences the kind of person you are. For example, if the kind of person I wish to be is a rich person, I make my decisions based on the principle of getting rich the fastest way possible. If I wish to be a loving person, I make decisions based on what I think will bring me to that goal. In previous chapters we have spent much time working to recover, re-member, and recognize the kind of person you were individually created to be. We have also encouraged you to consider what kind of goals you *were* living for and to *consciously choose* the kind of goals you wish to live for, to choose the direction you wish to travel.

Your ideas of what others think you are and how you define yourself are initially based on how your parents defined you by their actions of love or neglect toward you, combined with how you internalized their actions. If you internalized their neglect as your fault because of something you did wrong, this affects your path toward your desired goal. For example, if your goal is to be loving, and your parents always criticized you in whatever you tried to do, you may feel like you are failing constantly in your attempts to do anything loving. Some people get so discouraged by continuing the self-criticizing messages inside as adults that they define themselves as failures and give up on love. In doing this, they continue to invite their parents or parent substitutes (such as a critical spouse) to be their "coaches." Each of us has a choice: to *let go of* or to *embrace* our ability to direct and censor our own self-messages, to gently but firmly take back the charge of our own lives, to grasp the real definition of our worth.

The person you *actually are* is created by the choices you have made and are making this very moment. You show yourself *what you want* by *what you do*. When you choose to be your own coach and your own friend on a daily basis, you teach yourself that you are worth loving, protecting, and respecting. You actually give yourself the opportunity to powerfully direct your soul—this life of yours that has been given to you on loan from God—toward love.

As Christians we embrace the truth of our faith that the Holy Spirit of God is within us. He is "the one who comes alongside of us"[4] and works with us and within us to empower us to move toward the love of God. The Holy Spirit does not kick the critical parents or others out of our brains or out of our self-talk. God may reveal to us that their words are not in line with his words of love, yet he continues to love us by giving us freedom. He guides and teaches each of us constantly by the principles he set up in the world from the beginning, one being that we reap what we sow. If we have pain in our lives, it is always an indication that something is wanting or needs our attention, that some part of us is longing to be transformed or healed. When we do not choose love for ourselves, God leads us to love

189

through our pain. When we have nowhere else to go, sometimes the pain is the only thing left to motivate us to find the courage to let go of the critical self-messages and walk toward love.

When we are victims of force and abuse, this is a different kind of pain. In abuse we unjustly suffer the consequences of another person's unloving action of destruction. There is no excuse for this destruction—the pain is an indication of how unjust the act was. Even in such a horrible experience, we are not alone in our pain. The prophet Isaiah, 750 years before the birth of Jesus, reminds us of how Jesus, though innocent, suffered the consequences of each unloving, destructive act of humankind so that we could be redeemed and healed:

> He was despised and rejected by men,
>   a man of sorrows, and familiar with suffering.
> Like one from whom men hide their faces
>   he was despised, and we esteemed him not.
> Surely he took up our infirmities
>   and carried our sorrows,
> yet we considered him stricken by God,
>   smitten by him, and afflicted.
> But he was pierced for our transgressions,
>   he was crushed for our iniquities;
> the punishment that brought us peace was upon him,
>   and by his wounds we are healed.
> We all, like sheep, have gone astray,
>   each of us has turned to his own way;
> and the LORD has laid on him
>   the iniquity of us all.
>
> Isaiah 53:3–6 NIV

If you do not bring truth to the innermost parts of yourself, then you and all the team members within you cannot be set free. It is when you *know* the truth that the truth will set you free. Returning to the football team analogy, imagine that the inner workings of your desires, values, choices, and self-talk are all "members of a team" within you. Begin to look for parallels between the need for unity within to reach a desired goal and the unity you see in a winning football team.

About a month ago I (Paul) was having lunch with the chaplain of the Dallas Cowboys, John Weber. He told me something about their former coach Tom Landry, one of the best coaches who ever lived. Tom Landry had once said, "I've got one of the easiest jobs in the word. My job is to make these guys do what they don't want to do every day so that they can reach the goals they have dreamed about their whole lives." These guys did not *have to* do what the coach asked of them—they chose to and then realized their professional dreams. We can learn from this example to search out our thoughts and examine: What does it mean in my life to walk toward those goals? What kind of fears am I to face and what familiar but destructive patterns am I to let go of to get to that goal? Connect with your spiritual self, unify yourself toward this goal, let go of fear, and choose daily to walk toward love.

If you have a tendency toward perfectionism, remember that a good coach would not tell his players, "As soon as you make a mistake, I will hate you and fire you!" He doesn't demand perfection. Too much pressure and resentment would be built up in each player if that were the case. Instead he inspires his players to do their best. He sets up a practice schedule so that each of his players is given the opportunity to maximize his God-given athletic ability. He works the team hard and works hard with them. He does not have to be hard on them, but he can still be firm, unwavering, committed to producing a team that goes after their goal, united, accessing their full potential, playing to the best of their ability.

If you are resistant to self-knowledge or self-awareness, consider here why Mother Teresa, such a humble woman herself, encouraged it. An effective coach gets to know *every* member of his team. There is not one member who goes by him unnoticed. He knows the guys who are first string and the guys who are sitting on the bench. He knows each of their strengths and weaknesses and has all the players train hard because they contribute to achieving the goal. Just think about how confident you feel if you know that someone can fill in for your job if you have to call in sick. You do not want the whole project at work to be halted because of your unexpected absence. No one will do the job exactly like you, but you have trained backups who do their job with excellence, to fill in the gaps when things do not go exactly as planned. A football player can give his all during each game, with the confidence of knowing that if anything happens to him, the game can go on.

This team is a picture of the inner workings of your body, mind, and heart. You are a human being with a body and a soul. You are a spiritual being with emotions and thoughts. Mother Teresa and Saint Augustine emphasized knowing yourself and filling yourself in the same way that a coach knows and loves each of his players. He appreciates them and inspires them to pursue the goal the whole team wants. If you do not take the position as coach in your own life, then who will? You alone can fearlessly know all your strengths and weaknesses and commit to loving and inspiring your weaknesses to be united in love or to be let go. Who will be your coach if you do not respond to this invitation that you are offering yourself?

We pray, "The Lord is my Shepherd. I shall not be in want." God, like a shepherd, always wants to lead you to truth and to his love, but it is not God's job to do your work for you. It is God's job to love you thoroughly. Philippians 4:13 tells us, "I can do all things through Christ who strengthens me." When you invite God to do it, he will strengthen you to let go of the negative messages you repeat to yourself. What if a football coach went to the owner of the team and said, "Here! This whole group of people is yours; do whatever you want with them." The owner has already entrusted the team to the coach. He or she gives him all the freedom necessary to develop a good team.

God created you and gave you dominion over your own body. You are called to be a good steward or coach of your body, soul, and the gifts he gave you. You can choose to unite yourself with God and his purposes. I was so inspired the other day when I heard Dr. Laura Schlessinger on the radio saying, "Our lives are on loan to us by God to carry our souls through life." Our parents were the ones holding and teaching this loan of ourselves when we were young. We are the carriers now.

When you question your worth, consider a professional football team. Currently each team is worth approximately one billion dollars. We can easily understand the worth of a football team, but it is often difficult to grasp our own. You are of greater worth than any pro football team. God tells us in his Word: "Don't you know that your body is the temple of the Holy Spirit, who lives in you and was given to you by God? You do not belong to yourself, for God bought you with a high price" (1 Cor. 6:19–20 NLT). God uniquely designed and created each of us. Isaiah 49:16 teaches us that God inscribed each of us on the palm of his hand. God sent his only Son to offer us the perfection that he requires. As we read earlier, all of our imperfect actions, all actions that were or are not in accordance with love, have fallen on Jesus. If we could even begin to grasp what a high price the payment of God himself was to redeem us, we would understand that we are worth much more than a one-billion-dollar football team.

## Encouraging Each Part

In this chapter our focus is on your growth, developing your ability to unite yourself with love and toward love. You can commit to leading and loving yourself toward love by choosing to know the team members within, love them, and inspire them to be united. If one part of you will not be transformed, then let it go. This is the concept Jesus was teaching us when he said:

> If your right eye causes you to sin, pluck it out and cast it from you; for it is more profitable for you that one of your members perish, than for your whole body to be cast into hell. And if your right hand causes you to sin, cut it off and cast it from you; for it is more profitable for you that one of your members perish, than for your whole body to be cast into hell.
>
> Matthew 5:29–30

We are not encouraging you to pluck out your right eye, but if a player is not showing up to practice, if he has a constant attitude of apathy, if he is not unified with the goal that the whole team is going toward, the coach must ask the player to commit to the goal or leave. In the same way, it is important that you have a working communication with all of you, that you are consciously working on recovering an idea of what the true good is for each member of your inner team, and also that you have no fear of letting go of a part of yourself that refuses, absolutely refuses, to join with the other members in the direction of love.

The way I (Cheryl) think of this process is to speak the truth with love to the part of myself that does not want to be transformed. I encourage that part of me to join in pursuing the love that the rest of the members of my soul and body long for. If that member will not embrace love, then the most loving thing to do is to let that part go and continue traveling on. For example, you may choose to let go of the self-sabotaging part of yourself, like my father did that day in the parking lot of Dallas Theological Seminary.

My father reminded me today that research indicates that males, while forming in their mother's womb, are bathed with testosterone. Females have some testosterone but are not given nearly as much. When this testosterone bath occurs, the right brain begins to shrink some. This is the more intuitive or artistic side of our brain, the "relational" brain. The left side of our brain (which is relatively equal in size between males and females) is the more mathematical and logical side. In other words, my father said, "We men are born relationally brain damaged." This is perhaps why the research also indicates that married men do 300 percent better in overall health (less stress, fewer heart attacks, longer life) than single men. There is hardly any statistical difference in health when comparing married women to single women.

All this is to say that men *do* have the ability to form intimate connections, to love in relationships, and to think about relational ideas. It is just not *naturally* as easy for them as it is for women. I remember studying the brain in neuropsychology. It is phenomenal how the brain will work to compensate to fill in for what is missing if brain damage occurs. The left side of the brain will actually start doing some of the right brain's functions. So you see, I wrote the football analogy so that men can learn about relationships while they watch football! If they do not read anything in this book, perhaps we can share this concept with them and they will be responsive because a football team is involved! If not, of course we can graciously recognize that they have the freedom to choose for themselves.

## A Goal-Setting Exercise

1. Consider the following passage, found in Colossians 3:13–15, and what it means in your new commitment to know, love, and unite your team.

> Bear with each other and forgive whatever grievances you may have against one another. Forgive as the Lord forgave you. And over all these virtues put on love, which binds them all together in perfect unity. Let the peace of Christ rule in your hearts, since as members of one body you were called to peace (NIV).

2. Write down your idea of your main goal in life.
3. Write other goals you have set or want to set for yourself

   a. in your life
   b. in your marriage
   c. in your family
   d. at work (God bless the work of full-time moms! Reach out and encourage each other in this loving endeavor. As surely as you love your kids, you are loved deeply, and you are not alone.)

4. Prioritize your goals by their importance to you. Consider how to lovingly but firmly encourage and motivate your inner team to choose action in these areas. I found a beautiful quote on this chapter's subject from Leo Tolstoy:

> Remember that your understanding of your inner self holds the meaning of your life, and it makes you free if you do not force it to serve your flesh. The human soul which is

enlightened by understanding and freed from passions, and lit with the divine light, stands on a firm foundation.[5]

5. Look at your main goal in life and all your other goals. Are they in line with the deepest part of yourself as you get to know your true purpose here on earth?

Write down five real ways you can "coach" yourself and encourage yourself now, today. (For example, remind yourself that God, the owner of the football team, is not a critical father!)

If you have difficulty deciding on these, think of five ways you have wanted your spouse, your parents, or your friends to be there for you. Translate these things into action steps or words of encouragement you can give to yourself! If you wish, you can thank them for inspiring you to create a way to complete this exercise.

# twelve

# Creating an Unbreakable Bond with God

Continue seeking Him [God] with seriousness. Unless He wanted you, you would not be wanting Him.

C. S. Lewis

The end then of learning is to repair the ruins of our first parents by regaining to know God aright, and out of that knowledge to love Him, to imitate Him, to be like Him as we may the nearest, by possessing our souls of true virtue, which being united to the heavenly grace of faith, makes up the highest perfection.

John Milton

Forming an unbreakable bond with God is the most important connection you can make in your life. God invites you to enjoy a relationship with him. He pursues you. You also pursue him; we all do. In our deepest selves we have a recollection that we were created to be in relationship with the God who created us. As surely as an orphan seeks the love of his or her unknown mother and father, so we seek eternal love from God, our Father. "Our hearts are restless"[1] and our hearts desire rest. We seek to know God, unknown to us yet not unknowable. He is nearer than our next breath. He is constantly seeking us, consistently desiring to give us knowledge of himself and fill us with his love. He is Love. He waits for you and seeks an entrance into your heart.

God is not like anything else or anyone else who promises you love yet leaves you empty. Love does not abandon children. Love does not forsake his lover. If we are adults and we do not know God, it is because we have lost our way to him; he has not lost his way to us. We try to go our own way, hoping we will find the path back to Love. Yet we forget the way back to our true home: "For the desire for true good is planted by nature in the minds of men, only error leads them to stray towards false good."[2] We look for his love in the face of every person we encounter, yet we do not realize it is his love we are ultimately seeking. Love wants the *true good* for the object of his love. Until we awaken to the love that he offers, we abandon and forsake our very selves.

God desires that none should be lost, *not one* soul to be left without knowing his love. We invite you to take the time to get to know God, to embrace this opportunity to form a real and lasting relationship with him. Although you may begin an intimate (personal) relationship with God today, your relationship does not form overnight but is formed over time, like other relationships. Engage with us in this process of perfecting (growing toward maturity) your relationship with him and healing the wounds and misperceptions you have of him. We wish to share with you eleven key stepping-stones that you can use as tools to direct you in knowing God, experiencing his love, and building your relationship with him.

As humans we are given the privilege of having a higher calling than the animals. We have the ability to live above our instincts. We have a conscience, and we can think abstractly. We have the ability to reason and make choices in complicated situations. We have souls and thus we have the ability to live for deeper purposes than feeding our physical bodies. In Scripture we read that God has created each of us with the intention that we become holy: "For the purpose of God for you is this: that you may be holy" (1 Thess. 4:3).[3]

Mother Teresa expressed that this higher calling is God's greatest gift to us: "Holiness is the greatest gift that God can give us because for that reason He created us. . . . Determine to be holy because He is holy." She continued: "If we learn to love, we learn to be holy."[4] It is through learning what love is, connecting with the love our Creator has for us, and learning to love as he does in our own lives that we become holy. Connecting with your call to holiness connects you with the deepest purposes of your life. Since God's design and purpose for you is to be holy, you can freely invite him to work with you and within you as you grow more whole, more loving, and thus more holy.

We invite you to stop here for a moment and pray that God will reveal his love to you in the biggest way your heart can embrace. Ask God to work with you to create an inner safety so that you feel free to let go of your fear, so you can be flexible enough to enlarge your heart, so that you can embrace the endless supply of love he wants to give you.

## Eleven Stepping-Stones

*Undivided heart for God.* Cultivate unity within and direct yourself toward God and his purposes.

*No fear.* Perfect love casts out fear. Learn to approach God through his grace and let go of fear. Fear paralyzes us from moving forward, because fear has to do with punishment. Receive his forgiveness and love.

*Be in an attitude of prayer, always.* Prayer is your communication with God.

*Read the Holy Scriptures, which God gave to us.* They are love letters from him meant to enrich our lives by bringing truth to the innermost parts.

*Enlarge your heart.* Expand the territory of your heart so love has room to make its home.

*A*sk God to lead you. When the Lord is your Shepherd, you shall not want.

*K*now the real God. Let go of projections, expectations, and myths.

*A*ppoint a specific time to spend with God. Make time to cultivate your relationship with him. Find a local place of worship.

*B*uild safe relationships with others. Each person is created in God's image.

*L*isten to God. Cultivate silence in your life. Consider the ways God speaks to you.

*E*ternal perspective. Cultivate this perspective to prioritize what really matters.

Working through each of the eleven steps will help you build an unbreakable bond with God.

### Stepping-Stone 1: Undivided Heart for God

Cultivate unity within and direct yourself toward God and his purposes.

God's first commandment that he gave to us through Moses was to have an undivided heart for him: "You shall have no other gods before Me" (Exod. 20:3). We can learn what this means by reading a prayer of King David in the Psalms: "Teach me your way, O LORD, and I will walk in your truth; give me an undivided heart, that I may fear your name" (Ps. 86:11 NIV). David prays this because he is aware that his heart is easily led astray. He finds himself looking for love in all the wrong places. King David had slept with another man's wife, Bathsheba. He then had Bathsheba's husband sent out to battle with the clear intent of getting him killed. But David also was the shepherd boy who was not afraid to face the giant Goliath with only his slingshot and a few stones because Goliath was mocking God. When King Saul sought unjustly to kill David, David did not seek revenge, because he honored the fact that God had set Saul as king and he recognized it was God's place to remove him.

David was by no means perfect, yet he repented of his unloving acts. He wept and was truly broken inside when he realized what he had done and how unloving he had been by committing adultery with Bathsheba and murdering her husband. God later described David as "a man after my own heart" because of his continual persistence in seeking after God's heart and transforming his own love to be more like the love of God. David asked God to teach him the truth—"teach me your way"—so he could recover a clear picture of what the true good is.

King David asked God to cultivate in him an undivided heart so that he would "fear the name of God." We often overlook or just misunderstand this fear of God. In Proverbs 1:7 we read that the "fear of the LORD is the beginning of knowledge." If we wish to gain wisdom and gain understanding, we are to begin by "fearing the Lord." But what does this mean? This "fear" does not refer to a shaking terror of God but a reverence and an understanding of God's nature. To fear God is essentially to hallow his name. When we pray the Lord's Prayer, we pray, "Our Father in heaven, hallowed be your name" (Matt. 6:9). *Hallowed be your name* means "holy is your name." The holiness of God is to be worthy of complete devotion as one perfect in goodness and righteousness. When we pray this part of the Lord's Prayer we are communicating: "Eternal Father of all creation, we remember your name, your person, your nature. You are holy, you are love, you are perfect in goodness and righteousness. We are created in your image, that we may honor you and reflect you in all our thoughts and actions."

To understand that God is love, to hallow him, and to embrace that he knows what the true good is for each human soul and for each living creature on the earth is the beginning of wisdom. If we really had perfect faith at this moment and knew with our whole being that God is perfect in goodness and wants our best always, what would we ever be afraid of? We would seek him with our whole heart and follow his direction to the last letter because we would know that he will lead us only to more love. Consider the deep connection that Jesus had with the Father. He was willing to die for us and entrust himself to the will of his Father because he knew God's will was to reconcile us to his love.

Jesus was perfect in his love relationship with God. But King David was not perfect, nor are we perfect, not yet at least! One thing that we see a lot as a psychologist and a psychiatrist is the painful identity crisis that people face when they feel like they always have to portray a perfect image. We want others to think we have already arrived at forming an undivided heart. It is important that we let go of wearing a mask of perfection.

We sometimes want so much to project a good image of ourselves to others that we split off our "bad" parts and hide them away in darkness. When we continue to live behind a perfect-person mask, we confuse ourselves and start thinking we *are* already mature and perfected. We do not recognize that we still have a propensity to act out of the unloving parts hidden deep within us.

Remember what we worked on in the previous chapter. It is important to get to know *every member* on your inner team, the good players and "bad" players. Once you bring them all into the light of the locker room, then you inspire them and teach them the truth of how to get to the goal. The more we unify ourselves and become less split off and fragmented, the more we mature spiritually. This is not about comparing ourselves to others either. We have no idea what team members they started with. Remember that you cannot become perfectly whole or mature overnight. It takes time.

As you seek God's truth and his good way for your innermost parts, you build unity within yourself. You begin to create a whole person united with love and the purposes of a holy God.

Here is a prayer that Jesus prayed to God the Father on our behalf:

> Holy Father, keep them and care for them . . . so that they will be united just as we are. . . .
> Make them pure and holy by teaching them your words of truth. . . .

I have given them the glory you gave me, so that they may be one, as we are—I in them and you in me, all being perfected into one. . . . You love them as much as you love me. . . . You loved me even before the world began!

John 17:11, 17, 22–24 NLT

As you cultivate an undivided heart, remember that you are loved deeply. "You are forgiving and good, O Lord, abounding in love to all who call to you" (Ps. 86:5 NIV).

### *Stepping-Stone 2: No Fear*

Perfect love casts out fear. Learn to approach God through his grace and let go of fear. Fear paralyzes us from moving forward, because fear has to do with punishment. Receive his forgiveness and love.

Stepping-stones 1 and 2 seem to contradict each other, but they don't. They actually fit beautifully together. The "fear" in step one, as we just learned, is about reverence and honor, by which we recognize the holiness of God. The "fear" we are to let go of in step two comes from the verse "Perfect love casts out fear" (1 John 4:18), which has to do with accepting the grace offered to us by a holy God. God, who is perfect in love, is able to forgive you of your imperfections so that you can walk confidently (without fear) toward him to develop a relationship with him. God is a just judge. To understand the mercy of God and let go of our fear of his judgment, it is important for us to take a brief look at his justice.

If you want what is truly good, you learn to be *just* as well as merciful. In other words, if your ten-year-old daughter steals money from you, then—in order to truly love her—you set up a consequence to teach her that she is responsible for her action. In addition to the consequence you could also ask her what she wanted the money for and teach her how she can work around the house to *earn* money for herself (after she pays back the money she stole). Proverbs 22:6 encourages us to train children in the way they ought to go so that when they grow up they will not travel far off that path.

God also longs to train us and direct us toward that which is good. We have already focused on the first half of Proverbs 1:7: "The fear of the LORD is the beginning of knowledge." The second half reads: "But fools despise wisdom and instruction." We have the freedom to be foolish and reject the path of love that God offers us. It is ironic that God both offers us the path toward love and also gives us the freedom to reject that path. What is important to understand though is that a *just* God does not make up excuses for our foolishness or our wrongdoings. He does not say, "That's all right; you will do better next time." He does not say, "Well, over time I will forget about what you did." He does not say, "If you do ten good things, you can make up for the one unloving thing you just did." The Scripture is clear that we are each held accountable before God for every unloving act we have done, each unkind word we have spoken, and even each thought we have in our minds that is not in accordance with his perfect love. That alone would make any of us fear having a relationship with a just and holy God! Indeed we read in Scripture: "Who can say, 'I have made my heart clean, I am pure from my sin'?" (Prov. 20:9). "There is not a just man on earth who does good and does not sin" (Eccles. 7:20).

Sin and judgment, however, are only part of the truth. To become whole, we want the whole truth. The other part of God's love is his mercy and his grace. He offers us a way to approach him with confidence. Here we can discover how: "For God so loved the world that He gave His only begotten Son, that whoever believes in Him should not perish but have everlasting life. For God did not send His Son into the world to condemn the world, but that the world through Him might be saved" (John 3:16–17). This is not simply a Sunday school passage to memorize and never think about again. This is truth for our everyday lives: God wants us to be able to know him and approach him without fear. It is still a mystery to completely understand how he has done this, yet he has made a way that we are both *accountable* for our actions and also *forgiven* for our actions through the perfection of Jesus. God takes our debts and pays them through Christ, who was perfect and thus perfectly able to do it. God even hints of this a thousand years before Jesus took the form of a man here on this earth: "The LORD redeems his servants; no one will be condemned who takes refuge in him" (Ps. 34:22 NIV).

The Book of Job is regarded as the first book of the Bible ever written. Job illustrates most clearly this question of redemption and God's justice when he speaks about God's judgment and the fear involved:

> How can a mortal be righteous before God? . . .
> His wisdom is profound, his power is vast. . . .
> Though I were innocent, I could not answer him;
>     I could only plead with my Judge for mercy. . . .
> If only there were someone to arbitrate between us,
>     to lay his hand upon us both,
> someone to remove God's rod from me,
>     so that his terror would frighten me no more.
> Then I would speak up without fear of him,
>     but as it now stands with me, I cannot.
>
> Job 9:2, 4, 15, 33–35 NIV

God answered Job by providing a mediator who would lay his hands on both God and man to reconcile us together. In the Torah and the rest of the Old Testament we read how the children of Israel could approach God with confidence through the sacrifice of an innocent, perfect lamb. In the Book of Hebrews, we read:

> Just think how much more the blood of Christ will purify our hearts from deeds that lead to death so that we can worship the living God. For by the power of the eternal Spirit, Christ offered himself to God as a perfect sacrifice for our sins. That is why he is the one who mediates the new covenant between God and people, so that all who are invited can receive the eternal inheritance God has promised them. For Christ died to set them free from the penalty of the sins they had committed under that first covenant.
>
> Hebrews 9:14–15 NLT

The way we can let go of our fear and approach the perfect love of God is by accepting God's provision of his perfect love. These are profound truths found in Scripture that have been discussed in one-thousand-page books. This is stepping-stone 2, because it is clear that many of us do not approach forming a relationship with God for fear of his wrath and rejection. Fear is often the main thing that blocks us from love. Fear has to do with not feeling safe or protected. Sometimes we want love so much that we think we can get it by just throwing out the fear. When you teach yourself to ignore every warning of danger, you abandon the communication your soul would give you. When you do that, you often wind up jumping into a relationship with someone who is not safe! It is important not to shut down our fear response but to educate and direct it toward the truth when it is being irrational. It is important to understand that in perfect love there is no need to hold on to fear. God is the holder of perfect love, and he teaches us to love perfectly . . . but we are not perfect at it.

The important concept to understand in this second step is to learn how to invite God's perfect love into your heart so that you do not have to be afraid of coming before him to have a relationship with him. I do not think that any of us would really, if we were standing before God, throw caution to the wind and boldly say: "God, here I am. Search me and see if you can find anything unloving within me. I dare you, because I know that I am all love through and through, just like you."

We fear God for a reason. We now have the opportunity to cast that fear out completely and have no condemnation through the provision God has made to pay the consequences of our unloving acts through his perfect love. And not only that, but as we understand God's love, mercy, and grace and invite them into our lives, we will grow to have less fear in our relationships with ourselves and others. The more we surround ourselves with God's love, the less we try to form relationships with people who are not safe and who are continuously unloving. The more we surround ourselves with the love of God, the more we can minister to others who are hurting because of their lack of love.

If you are having difficulty understanding these concepts, ask God to give you insight. Go to a pastor or a church and ask for clarification. Start reading the Bible and begin to understand how it applies to your daily existence and the development of your psychological health (your soul's wholeness) and spiritual life. Begin to know how you can approach God without fear.

### Stepping-Stone 3: Be in an Attitude of Prayer, Always

Prayer is your communication with God.

The Bible encourages us to pray without ceasing (1 Thess. 5:17). That does not mean we spend every waking moment of every day on our knees. God's intention for us is to love him, love each other, confess our faults to one another, encourage each other, and speak the truth in love. If we are praying all day in our rooms, we won't have time to do any of the other things God intended for our good and for us to enjoy. Imagine if Jesus were always praying and said to his friends and others, "Go away. I don't have time for you. I am praying!"

To pray without ceasing means to be in an attitude of prayer all day every day. To pray without ceasing is to put love into action, to do everything in love. It also means we are to carry on a lifelong conversation with God in our minds in the midst of our daily lives.

For example, I may say to God, "See what I am thinking now. Can you believe that I was thinking that way? Teach me to direct that part of myself toward real love." Or "Look at that beautiful field of wildflowers. I so appreciate that you created such beauty." Or "God, I am feeling so discouraged and awful right now. Teach me where I can find true courage. Encourage me and teach me how to encourage myself." Or "God, give me wisdom to work with this person in this situation. Give me wisdom to ease her pain and teach her how to truly love and protect herself." Or "God, I am really mad at you right now for letting _____ die, or for letting _____ develop that disease, or for letting _____ be abused. I realize I am angry at you because I do not see the whole picture. I do not understand

207

your gift of free will to all of us who misuse it daily. Give me understanding *now*, please! But if you won't show me now, then give me trust, patience, a forgiving attitude, and wisdom until I get to heaven and you can tell me what it all means."

Some of us may not be so soft-spoken with God, but he can handle it. Be real with him in every situation. It may seem weird at first as your relationship with God changes, but it is real, and as in any relationship, you are changed by his love and by interactions with him.

It is important to create a time to pray besides just talking to him throughout the day. After a time of being open and honest with God, you long for the time you can spend talking to him—just as you would be drawn to the phone to call a good friend.

Praise God, not because he needs to be fed with our praises, because God is not in need of anything, but because we were created to worship—to admire beauty, truth, and all that is lovely. Confess to God the ways you keep yourself from loving him, others, and yourself. Petition God on behalf of others who are suffering in our world, in your home, in your city, in your country. Pray for leaders that they will be just and gain wisdom. Pray for God's direction and protection in your own life as you seek to follow his loving example. Pray for everything, or for anything, without ceasing.

### Stepping-Stone 4: Read the Holy Scriptures, Which God Gave to Us

The Scriptures are love letters from God meant to enrich our lives by bringing truth to the innermost parts.

The Bible is God's gift to us. In it we read, "Every word of God is flawless; he is a shield to those who take refuge in him" (Prov. 30:5 NIV). The Bible is God's love letter for us to read and understand about his nature, the nature of the world around us, and our own human nature. Hebrews 4:12 says the Word of God is living and powerful, and sharper than any two-edged sword. It is able to reveal to us our unconscious thoughts. God's words are a searchlight into our soul. They reveal our innermost parts that we would not otherwise see. Just as when you have a love relationship with another person, you learn from them, so also you learn from the words of God, through his communication back to you. You see yourself in ways you had never seen. You learn more about yourself and how to change yourself to be more loving. You see parts of yourself that you don't see when you are alone. Sometimes it is a reality that you do *not* want to see, but it causes you to grow. Your ability to love travels to a deeper level than you would have gone to on your own.

Also, consider, if your lover were on a trip and wrote you a long love letter expressing his or her innermost thoughts and feelings as well as what he or she was thinking about you, wouldn't you want to read it as soon as you possibly could? You would not only read it but meditate on it and use it to build an intimate relationship with your lover. This is what God has given to us. He is our lover and we are his bride. That is the analogy he chose to describe his relationship with us.

There is nothing you can do that will be more powerful in your life than meditating daily on Scripture. Meditating is not merely reading the Bible but reading it until a principle hits you between the eyes. You jot down that passage on a piece of paper or note card and carry it around with you for as long as you need to really understand it. When you meditate on it, you will actually change your way of thinking and behaving as a result of that passage. In addition to these benefits, God also designed us so that we actually improve our health when we meditate. Scientific research is now revealing that meditation lowers your blood pressure, lowers your anxiety level, and improves your overall health.

In early childhood both of us were taught this principle of meditating on Scripture daily. We both think that it has been one of the most important stepping-stones in our lives for the continuous need we have to recover a clear view of what is true, good, and most loving. Through the words of God, who created us to be in relationship, we learn to build the unbreakable bonds we desire with him, others, and ourselves.

### *Stepping-Stone 5: Enlarge Your Heart*

Expand the territory of your heart so love has room to make its home.

In biblical terms your heart is your mind, emotions, and will. Your heart is like your soul. It is the deepest part of you, the part of you that longs for intimate connections. In Revelation 3:20 we read that God is always standing at your heart's door knocking, asking you to invite him in so that he can become intimately involved in your life. He loves you now, regardless of whatever sins you have committed in your lifetime (remember King David?). The following is a real example of his love for the people he has created:

Jesus loved the people of Jerusalem—he went there to personally tell them how they could have an intimate relationship with him and inherit eternal life. After they rejected Jesus, he walked to the outskirts of the city and wept and cried out in heavy sadness. Earlier he had lovingly said, "O Jerusalem, Jerusalem. . . . How often I wanted to gather your children together, as a hen gathers her brood under her wings, but you were not willing!" (Luke 13:34).

In a hailstorm a mother hen instinctively loves her little baby chicks so much that she will hold out her wings and the chicks will run under them, and their lives will be saved, though the mother may die from the hailstones hitting her on the head. That is the picture of the deep love of God. This is the way Jesus chose to express how he feels about the people he loves. How sad he is when we choose to reject him! God loves us and wants us to accept him, but he does not *need* us to accept him. God is self-sustaining, so he does not come to us out of any kind of neediness. We read in the Scriptures that he chose out of his own good pleasure to give us life. He freely offers us his love and calls us to himself. He created each of us to become whole, so he offers us this deeper call to holiness and gives us the love and ability to follow this calling.

It may be difficult for you to offer your heart to him because of misperceptions you have about him or about yourself. God may have greatly disappointed you in some of your expectations of him. You may feel unworthy of his love. But he reminds us in the Scriptures that the more unworthy we are, the more he wants us. In one parable Jesus described how God is like a shepherd who left the ninety-nine sheep that were safe to go and find the one sheep that was lost.

We read in 1 Chronicles 4:10 the prayer of a man named Jabez: "And Jabez called on the God of Israel saying, 'Oh, that You would bless me indeed, and enlarge my territory, that Your hand would be with me, and that You would keep me from evil, that I may not cause pain!' So God granted him what he requested." Here we can learn from Jabez's prayer that we too can ask God to enlarge the territory *of our hearts*, that he may bless us with himself.

The apostle Paul writes his own prayer for our hearts to be enlarged by faith so we can begin to grasp how wide and long and high and deep the love of Christ is, and to know his love, which surpasses knowledge:

> For this reason I kneel before the Father, from whom his whole family in heaven and on earth derives its name. I pray that out of his glorious riches he may strengthen you with power through his Spirit in your inner being, so that Christ may dwell in your hearts through faith. And I pray that you, being rooted and established in love, . . . may be filled to the measure of all the fullness of God.
>
> Now to him who is able to do immeasurably more than all we ask or imagine, according to his power that is at work within us, to him be glory . . . for ever and ever! Amen.
>
> Ephesians 3:14–21 NIV

Remember, we do not have to be perfect, nor can we be perfect here on earth. It may be difficult for you to let God in for a variety of psychological and spiritual reasons, but he is able to give you the ability to open your heart to him and enlarge your heart to embrace his love. He waits for you to invite him.

### Stepping-Stone 6: Ask God to Lead You

When the Lord is your Shepherd, you shall not want.

Ask God to lead you. If God is Love, who else would we want to follow but Love himself? We have a choice as to where our heart is, what our goals are, and where we take ourselves. We read in another psalm of David: "Teach me to do Your will, for You are my God; Your Spirit is good. Lead me in the land of uprightness" (Ps. 143:10).

It is amazing also to read in the New Testament that there was a time when Jesus asked his disciples if they wanted to leave him. He was speaking about something that was difficult to understand, saying: "I am the bread of life! Your ancestors ate manna in the wilderness, but they all died. However, the bread from heaven gives eternal life to everyone who eats it" (John 6:48–50 NLT). The passage continues:

> Even his disciples said, "This is very hard to understand. How can anyone accept it?"
>
> Jesus knew within himself that his disciples were complaining, so he said to them, "Does this offend you? . . . It is the Spirit who gives eternal life. Human effort accomplishes nothing. And the very words I have spoken to you are spirit and life." . . .
>
> At this point many of his disciples turned away and deserted him. Then Jesus turned to the Twelve and asked, "Are you going to leave, too?"
>
> Simon Peter replied, "Lord, to whom would we go? You alone have the words that give eternal life. We believe them, and we know you are the Holy One of God."
>
> verses 60–69

When we ask God to lead us, we are stepping out in faith that he is Love and will lead us toward all that is loving. We learned in stepping-stone 2 that there is no fear in love. The more you understand the reality that you can be surrounded right now by God's perfect love, the less you will have reason to worry about all the circumstances and problems that happen in your life. Kierkegaard says, "Besides God, what else do I need?" and quotes Matthew 16:26:

"For what would it profit a person if he gained the whole world, but damaged his own soul; what should he have in return?"

. . . The antithesis would read something like this: What damage would there be to a person if he lost the whole world and yet did not damage his soul; what would he need in return?[5]

If a woman or man felt truly and utterly loved by a perfect love for all eternity, what more would she or he need? Indeed, if we have God and are led by his loving direction, it truly is as Jesus says: We do not have anything to worry about.

> Therefore I tell you, do not worry about your life, what you will eat or drink; or about your body, what you will wear. Is not life more important than food, and the body more important than clothes? Look at the birds of the air; they do not sow or reap or store away in barns, and yet your heavenly Father feeds them. Are you not much more valuable than they? Who of you by worrying can add a single hour to his life? . . .
>
> So do not worry, saying, "What shall we eat?" or "What shall we drink?" or "What shall we wear?" For the pagans run after all these things, and your heavenly Father knows that you need them. *But seek first his kingdom and his righteousness, and all these things will be given to you as well.*
>
> Matthew 6:25–27, 31–33 NIV, emphasis added

It is easy to say, "Ask God to lead you," but it is more difficult for us to really invite him to do this leading. The more chaotic our childhood was, the more we felt out of control. The more we felt out of control growing up because a parent was an alcoholic, neglectful, abusive, or overly controlling, the more controlling we often became to compensate for feeling so out of control growing up. When we stop and look at our lives, though, and become deeply honest with ourselves, we can begin to see choices we have made that didn't give us the love we truly desired. They ended up being more of a quick fix instead of a true good. God is above time. The Scriptures tell us that a day is like a thousand years to him and a thousand years are like a

213

day. God does not give us a quick fix unless a quick fix is really the truest good for us.

It is important to learn how to trust God and be open and honest with him about all the ways we do not feel protected by him. It was God who designed us; he always wants what is truly best for us, and he always knows what is truly best for us. As we learn to seek him and the wisdom he wants to give us, we will grow from his love and begin to be unafraid to share his limitless love with others. As we invite God to lead us to be more like him, he teaches us how to lead ourselves with more wisdom, love, and grace.

### Stepping-Stone 7: Know the Real God

Let go of myths, projections, and expectations.

Unless we take the time to know who God really is, we just automatically hold on to whatever our parents, our culture, television, our schools, or our friends have taught us. We often interpret our own experiences of God based on what other people taught us about him. If Grandpa Joe told you that you broke your leg because you skipped out on school one day a year before it happened, then you may begin to think God just randomly punishes you whenever he feels like it. You may see God as some big judge in the sky, and you haven't ever considered that he is loving and merciful, seeking to have a personal relationship with you. One of the names of God that we find in Genesis is El Shaddai (17:1), which literally means "the Breasted One" or "God the sustainer of his people." We read in Isaiah: "[And the Lord answered], Can a woman forget her nursing child, that she should not have compassion on the son of her womb? Yes, they may forget, yet I will not forget you" (Isa. 49:15 AMP).

The Messiah is described as both a lamb and a lion. Whenever the Old Testament describes the Messiah who would come someday, it describes him in two different terms. We read in Hosea that the Messiah would come twice to the earth. He would come once as a meek lamb, a sacrifice for the sins of the world (see also Isaiah 53), but he will also come as a roaring lion to conquer the world and rule the world someday. Hosea

6:3 says he will come for a former rain (implying his first coming) and a latter rain (implying his second coming), and that the Jewish people would be scattered out of their land for two days (two periods of time) in between his comings. God's calling his Son a lion and a lamb is helpful for us to understand the multifaceted nature of God (Father, Son, and Holy Spirit).

In Matthew 3:17 we read that when John the Baptist baptized his cousin Jesus, the Father spoke aloud to the crowd from heaven and said, "This is My beloved Son, in whom I am well pleased." At the same moment the Holy Spirit took on the form of a dove and landed on Jesus' shoulder. At this one time we see the Father, Son, and Holy Spirit interacting with each other.

God is infinite. Thus there is always more we can know about who he is. He is much more than all the pat answers you may have heard when you were a child. It is important to realize that we only know a tiny fraction of him. This does not mean that all of a sudden we will find out God is unjust and unloving. You can date a person for three years, know him for six years before that, and still you will always learn more about this person if you marry him. This same person, however, unless he has perfected a very thorough mask from childhood, is not going to have a totally different character than the one you have known. God is even more unchanging than we are. He does not change, but our perspective of him does, because we grow in our understanding of him.

I (Cheryl) wrote my doctoral thesis on the misperceptions people have about God. It was amazing to read the results of different studies in all sorts of nonreligious journals. The overwhelming majority of them indicated that up to 85 percent of our perception of God is formed by how we experienced our own parents. If our dads or moms were cold, distant, and demanding, we usually describe God as cold, distant, and demanding. If our parents abused us in any way, we also think that God does not respect our boundaries and will take whatever he wants from us or do anything he wants to us in a selfish, abusive way. If our parents told us they loved us all the time yet showed us by their actions that they didn't have that much time for us, we begin to think that God loves us from a distance but just does not have time for us. Imagine also how if our parents spoiled us and gave us everything we wanted without any discretion as to what was truly good for us at the time—then we get very angry and resentful at God when he gives us consequences for our actions or says no to us when something we want is not going to bring us closer to love.

It is important we learn to let go of projecting our understanding and experience of our parents onto the living God. It is important that we give him a chance—and get to know him for who he really is. Just as we work to let go of any prejudice or stereotypes we may hold in our hearts so we can really get to know a person for who she or he is individually, so also it is important to let go of the baggage we throw onto God and get to know him.

I (Paul) hosted a live talk show recently, and a woman called in to complain about her husband. "He is really nice most of the time," she said, "except when he catches me telling our seven-year-old daughter about God; then he gets furious." She expected me to be critical of her husband and to feel sorry for her. I did feel sorry for her, but she was shocked when my reply was, "I *really* feel sorry for your husband."

"Why?" she asked.

I replied to her lovingly, "He must have been badly hurt and abandoned by his parents as a child, or else he wouldn't have so much projected hostility toward a God he doesn't even believe exists."

"Why yes!" she replied, astonished. "His parents were abusive and abandoned him at age four, and he grew up in an orphanage."

Please take a moment now to consider how your parents have influenced your understanding of God's nature. And then think about your expectations. We can expect with all confidence that God will keep his promises. God is true to his covenants with his people. God's promises are scattered throughout the whole Bible. There are books with just God's promises all outlined. It is wonderful to see all of the things God promises us: "May your unfailing love come to me, O LORD, your salvation according to your promise" (Ps. 119:41 NIV).

The problem is that God's unfailing love does not always look like the unfailing love that we wanted! It will never fail to be love, real love in its highest form, but we may fail to recognize it as love. We sometimes want God to be our genie, and we get mad if he isn't. I (Cheryl) remember a time in my life when I was praying that God would literally send me tablets of stone to tell me what to do, and I kept getting mad at God that he gave me the freedom to discover who I am, what I am gifted at, and what I would like to do with my life. I so wanted God to just tell me what to do. Now, looking back, I think it was because I was scared that I would do the "wrong" thing, and I thought that he would get mad at me. Or I wanted God to just tell me so that I could get mad at him if it didn't turn out right later on down the road. I would have someone to blame it on. God was giving me an opportunity to discover who I was created to be.

Earlier we saw that Ephesians 2:10 says that we are God's poem or an art masterpiece in his hands. We are each unique. We are creating the poem of ourselves, and yet God is always there with perfect rhythm, with all the words of every language to give to us or for us to discover. He wants to make us beautiful, lovelier, truer, so we bring more love into the world. This is not the mean dictatorlike God I was asking for! It just took some time and some patience with God—and of course he showed patience with me in the process—so that I could understand that God is bigger than my perception of him! He wanted to give me more than what I was expecting from him. One of my very favorite quotes after that experience—which I often return to—is this one by C. S. Lewis from a book aptly titled *The Weight of Glory:*

> Our Lord finds our desires, not too strong, but too weak. We are half-hearted creatures, fooling around with drink and sex and ambition when infinite Joy is offered us, like an ignorant child who wants to go on making mud pies in a slum because he cannot imagine what is meant by the offer of a holiday at sea. We are far too easily pleased.[6]

God wants to give us so much more than we can ask. Still, there is no mistake; there is pain in this world. We live in a world where people are given the freedom to choose to follow love or to twist love. We live in a fallen world. Yet Adam and Eve did not eat of the tree of eternal life. The Book of Genesis says that they were kept from that tree, and angels are still guarding it now, protecting us so that we do not live here forever in a fallen state. Because of that we all die eventually. Even though death is God bestowing his grace to us, losing someone to death is still painful. We all experience or know someone who experiences genetic disorders, diseases, cancer, starvation, and all sorts of natural disasters. In addition to these pains we experience man-made horrors such as September 11, 2001, the Holocaust, and wars in which innocent people are killed. It is difficult to understand, and some of it cannot ever be completely understood during our time here on earth.

It is important that we learn to talk to God about our disappointments and also learn to let go of unrealistic expectations such as, "If God loves me, he will not give me any life-threatening diseases." God may love you so much that he wants to give you the opportunity to slow down and develop an even deeper understanding of love. He may have allowed you to get a disease simply because it was genetically carried through your parents' genes. No one is saying that it is not a struggle to deal with difficult things, but we must know that God is there. He does not leave us alone in our pain. God became flesh and lived among us.[7] Jesus wore a crown of thorns, and, though innocent, was nailed on a cross for us. Who can comprehend the love of Jesus when he said, "Father, forgive them, for they do not know what they are doing" (Luke 23:34 NIV). Get to know the real God, not just your earthly father-projection or mother-projection.

### Stepping-Stone 8: Appoint a Specific Time to Spend with God

Make time to cultivate your relationship with God. Find a local place of worship.

If we do not choose to appoint a specific time to spend developing our relationship with God and our spiritual self, we will become more like the world and less like God, less directed, less purposeful, and less full in our inner self. God made us to be in relationship with him. Jesus uses the analogy of the vine. God is the vine and we are the branches. It is important that we live in him and he in us, so that we mature and develop spiritually. The way my grandmother would always talk to me about this concept was to imagine I have two dogs inside of me. One dog is the dog that wants all the quick fixes and all the earthly pleasures. It doesn't really care about anyone's true good. The other dog is my spiritual self who desires the will of God. Grandma would say, "Cheryl, you've got to feed that spiritual dog or else it will be starving! Otherwise that quick-fix dog is going to get so big from all the food it will just weigh you down and keep you sitting on that couch all day every day."

The main lesson to learn about feeding ourselves spiritually and forming an intimate relationship with God is to *do it!* Think about how we can forget to eat when we are in the middle of work. When we do not set aside a time to eat, we get really hungry later. Then we don't eat well because we just focus on taking away the hunger pains.

We hunger spiritually all the time, just as we hunger physically. We just do not usually cultivate our ability to recognize this hunger. We are spiritual beings, not just physical bodies. We starve ourselves spiritually when we forget to make time for God, to welcome his grace, to learn the ways of love, to direct ourselves to deeper purposes, to create deeper meaning in our lives, to understand our actions in relation to eternity, and to spend time with others who can encourage us as they are walking with the same purpose. When we starve our souls, we feel really hungry and needy. We are more likely to start reaching for anything that will make us feel good inside. We forget that God loves us, so we become discouraged.

Set aside a specific time to spend talking to God, reading his words, listening to him, learning from a pastor, priest, or respected teacher at your place of worship who studies God's Word, and meeting with other people who also pursue the ways of love. Set aside a specific time to invite God's grace and love to fill you, his wisdom to guide you, and his courage to empower you.

### Stepping-Stone 9: Build Safe Relationships with Others

Each person is created in God's image.

One of the best ways to understand God better and to become more intimate with him is to understand and become intimate with "God in skin." What does this mean? Well, as we have learned, God created humankind in his image. God didn't have a body, so he didn't make us to look physically like him. "In his image" must mean in his spirit or character. Since we are made in the image of God, we can learn to love the things he loves and hate the things he hates. We can do so many wonderful things because he gave us a soul, a spiritual self, and a complex brain with the ability to think and experience emotions. When you build relationships with safe, godly people, you are discovering more and more what it is like to have a relationship with God himself. When you treat yourself with the same love and respect God intended, you get to know him better. To love is to be like God is, because he is Love. Your relationships with others and within yourself do not replace your relationship with God. They enhance it.

We all have wrong beliefs about ourselves. We all have insecurities. We all have times when we feel like rejecting ourselves. James 5:16 tells us that if we confess our faults one to another, we will be healed. When we spend quality time week after week with people who love us unconditionally, who have an attitude of grace toward our failures, we develop a healthier and more accurate self-concept. We learn to see ourselves as God sees us. The formula that our friends Dr. Henry Cloud and Dr. John Townsend write about so often in their books on spiritual maturity is "Grace + Love + Time with loving friends results in spiritual maturity." We were created to be in relationship with others. We can know the love of God more through the love we are able to share with our friends and with ourselves.

### *Stepping-Stone 10: Listen to God*

Cultivate silence in your life. Consider the ways God speaks to you.

Many of us have forgotten what it is to stop, to actually have an amount of time that is filled with nothing but silence. Yet when we quiet our hearts and minds, we unearth the truths that were just waiting for a quiet time so that they could come to the surface. God speaks to us in a variety of ways. He speaks to us from his Word, from the conviction of the Holy Spirit, from circumstances, through others, through dreams, through the beauty of a sunrise or the seasons in nature. Sometimes we hear him teaching us through our painful experiences in life. He communicates in all kinds of ways.

In stepping-stone 9 we learned that God teaches us and communicates to us through our intimate relationships with other people. Verse 14 in Proverbs 11 tells us that in a multitude of counselors there is safety. God wants us to seek counsel from other wise people so he can speak through them. He could do anything he wants without people, but he chooses to give us the gift of others to help us hear what his truth is.

It is important that we interpret all that we *think* God is telling us in light of Scripture. If we think God is telling us to do something, yet it contradicts Scripture, then it is not of him. We are reminded in Isaiah 8:19 and 1 John 4:1 to test the spirits to see whether they are of God. It is important not to attribute every crack in the sidewalk you encounter or every communication you hear as God speaking to you. It may be some part of your subconscious, it may be some leftover voice of your parents, it may be an evil spirit, or it may be God.

I (Paul) have met many married couples where the husband prior to marriage walked up to his future wife and said, "God told me to marry you," and the wife was naive enough to believe him. Then after a few months of being married, or in some cases, a few days, she realizes that it may not have been God's voice after all, or she thinks, "God doesn't like me very much if it *was* his voice!"

Occasionally, when I taught future pastors at Dallas Theological Seminary, a student would walk up to me and say, "God is telling me to marry _____."

I would then ask him, "How do you know that?"

His reply would be, "I can feel it in my gut."

I would then reply, "How do you know it isn't indigestion?"

The student would get mad at me and walk away or realize he was interpreting his own feelings as God's direct call. This is why it is important, when we are listening and cultivating silence, to discern whether we hear God, our subconscious, or an evil force. It is important to be humble enough to admit that sometimes we don't really know. The best thing to do is to compare what we *think* God is telling us with Scripture to be sure it agrees and then to check out what we believe with other godly and truly wise people.

Another method of listening to God that is mentioned 150 times in Scripture is paying attention to our dreams. Again, it is important that we do not overinterpret but still learn from the way God created us. He didn't create us to have dreams for no reason. As we look at our dreams objectively, we can see them as a picture of what our subconscious is trying to work out deep within our soul.

Several years back, Henry Blackaby, author of the best-seller *Experiencing God*, joined us on our national radio broadcast. I (Paul) took a half day off work the day before to read the whole book. I was delighted with the things I read about experiencing God. That night I woke up with an intense dream, probably the most beautiful dream I have ever had in my life. In the dream I was taking an enjoyable walk through the woods by myself. I could smell the fragrance of the flowers and hear the birds singing and see the sun shining through the leaves of the trees. Then all of a sudden, when I thought I was all alone, I heard a male voice shouting, "Boo!" I was startled and jumped and turned around in fear, and Jesus was standing there in his robe, laughing at the fact that he had just teased me as a friend would. He came up to me and put his arm around me, on my shoulder, and walked through the woods with me.

I cherish the dreams that I have and remember. Job taught us that God speaks to us in the night seasons. Even our bad dreams can be good dreams if we use them to teach us about hidden anger or fear. Every action in every dream has meaning. I hope that some of you will have dreams about God or about what ways he wants more love to be in your life and your heart after reading this book. Pay attention to your dreams, cultivate silence in your daily life, and listen to God, because he wants to communicate to you.

### *Stepping-Stone 11: Eternal Perspective*

Cultivate an eternal perspective to prioritize what really matters.

To think long-range about the eternal nature of our souls and the souls of those around us, we have to really invest time and energy. In Matthew 6:33 Jesus encourages us to "Seek first the kingdom of God and His righteousness, and all these things shall be added to you." In today's world we rush to seek first whatever is popular, valued, or perceived to be a need. We forget the higher calling of our souls, which, when we remember, can add purpose and meaning to all of our other daily circumstances.

In the early 1990s the Dallas Cowboys beat the Pittsburgh Steelers in the Super Bowl. Since I (Paul) live in Dallas and sometimes lead their Bible studies, I am an avid Dallas Cowboys fan. I was very excited when one of the players, Chad Hennings, called me on the phone two weeks before the Super Bowl to ask me to join him for lunch. I thought he was probably nervous about the game and wanted me to calm him down or give him some psychiatric tips. I was proud of myself, thinking I might help the Dallas Cowboys win because of this lunch. When I got to the Mexican restaurant and met with Chad, I was disappointed at Chad's answer when I asked him what he wanted to talk about. "Bible prophecy," he answered.

I had written some fiction about Bible prophecy and had done a few of the Bible studies with the Dallas Cowboys on that topic, but I was disappointed because *I* wanted to talk about the Super Bowl game. Even though he had his own agenda, I asked him, "Aren't you excited about being on a Super Bowl team?"

"Sure, Paul, I am excited about being on a Super Bowl team," Chad replied. "But I am a lot more excited about being on the Kingdom team! Tell me what is going on in the world and what hints you gather from these things about God's future plans, because I want to be sure to fit in with his plans."

I was humbled by my friend Chad that day. I was more excited about the Super Bowl team than the Kingdom team, at least on that day. But every day when I wake up, I pray the prayers that I shared with you in the earlier chapter on practicing the art of love: "Help me become more like you and know you better today, God. Help me to serve you today. Help me to stay out of trouble today, because you know how unloving I can be. And help me to listen to you today and learn from anything that may go wrong today. I expect for some things to go wrong, but when they do, help me use them to learn and grow."

It is really when we take the time to cultivate an eternal perspective like that of Chad Hennings and daily remind ourselves of our deeper purposes for being here on this earth that we begin to see everything that happens in the world around us and in our own lives with an eternal perspective. It helps us realize that God is ultimately in control and that Love will reign in the end and for eternity. As we realize that God wants to provide for us and does not want us to be consumed with the worries of daily life, we can begin to understand and direct ourselves toward the most fulfilling purposes on earth. We can love as God's love is already abounding in heaven.

As Christians we are promised that there still may be many tribulations and afflictions here on earth, yet God will surely work with us to teach us so that we can learn and grow from each one of them. Jesus invites us to cultivate an eternal perspective so that we give ourselves the opportunity to store up for ourselves treasures in heaven where moth and rust do not destroy and no one can steal these treasures from us. We also develop maturity from our temporary trials here on earth. We learn how to love better, how to forgive more deeply, and how to seek God's grace and mercy in our own lives. We learn that

God can use unloving choices or horrible circumstances to make us into more loving people.

## Bond with God

I (Paul) was training some of my therapists at a staff meeting recently when one of them apologized for crying in front of a patient when she heard his horrible accounts of being abused as a child.

"Don't apologize!" I told her. "You cried because you were made in the image of God and had love and compassion for your patient. Your tears were more powerful than anything you could have told him about how important he is to God and how much God empathizes with his pain, because he sees God in you."

As you move toward God, you will see that his love transforms you and fills you. From experiencing and knowing his deep love for you, you learn to love yourself and generously give this love back to him and to others. He created us to form an unbreakable bond with him so that we can share his love and form unbreakable bonds with others.

## Wrapping Up

Each of the stepping-stones we presented are based on spiritual truths from the Bible. We invite you not to be overwhelmed by these eleven stepping-stones but instead to keep in mind the one unifying purpose underneath all of them. This purpose is to learn what it is to experience the fullness of God's love and to love him in return, as we were created to do. One of our favorite verses sums up the relationship God desires for us to have with him and with others: "He has shown you, O man, what is good; and what does the Lord require of you but to do justly, to love mercy, and to walk humbly with your God?" (Micah 6:8).

We can see that he wants us to protect ourselves and the justice of the innocent others who cannot protect themselves. He wants us to embrace mercy, showing forgiveness and kindness to those who have wronged us. Essentially, he wants us to want the true good for all and to learn what it is to humbly walk beside him in a loving relationship. God is always present. You can begin to pray for and cultivate an awareness of his presence, a knowledge of him, and a love relationship with him for all eternity.

# thirteen

# Final Considerations on Your Journey toward Love

There is no created being who can know how much and how sweetly and how tenderly the Creator loves us. And therefore we can with his grace and his help persevere in spiritual contemplation, with endless wonder at this high, surpassing, immeasurable love which our Lord in his goodness has for us; and therefore we may with reverence ask from our lover all that we will, for our natural will is to have God, and God's good will is to have us, and we can never stop willing or loving until the time comes that we shall be filled full in heaven.

Julian of Norwich

We are here to be witnesses of love and to celebrate life, because life has been created in the image of God. Life is to love and be loved.

Mother Teresa

Many of you will begin forming deeper relationships, unbreakable bonds, from applying to your life the insights you have learned from this book. Others of you will start walking toward these closer relationships and then realize that you have deeper, unresolved emotional blocks that ask for more love and attention than a book can give you. It is important for you to find a therapist who shares your faith or find a pastor, a counselor, or another kind of professional who will work with you to arrive at a place where you can let go of these barriers to love. A few of you (about 10–15 percent of the population) will be able to more fully carry out these insights only after you find appropriate medications for any genetic disorder or combination of genetic disorders that may be inhibiting your knowing God, others, and yourself intimately. This is an important truth that we did not want to leave out.

## Biological Blocks to Love

Some biological imbalances in our brains keep us from forming a deep connection with God, self, and others. Here is a brief description of the main genetic problems we may face.

Extreme genetic *perfectionism* (sometimes labeled obsessive compulsive disorder) will result in self-condemnation and the assumption that God utterly rejects you when you fail. Just as a person can be born with eyesight that is not 20/20, we can be born with brain chemicals that are slightly or largely off balance. We have no problem giving our children glasses so they can read. It is important that we care for our emotional selves with the same kind of love. If you think you may have a genetic imbalance, find a good psychiatrist and get the right medication to normalize it.

A few years ago a young woman flew to our day program from a distant country. She had a lifelong genetic obsessive compulsive disorder. She was filled with depression and constant self-critical messages. When we got her on a serotonin-correcting medicine (like Effexor-XR, Zoloft, or Celexa), then she was completely normal. She returned home and enjoyed life, enjoyed her friendships, and felt like she could now experience God's love. Her family was both surprised and excited about the results, because they had tried everything before this. (When you have a genetic imbalance such as this, even the positive effects of therapy will be blocked in many ways by the extreme self-critical messages.)

The tragic part of this story is that this young woman was involved in a church that was ignorant of the ways God could use medicine to heal people's psychological brain imbalances. Her church had taken a verse about "the sufficiency of Christ" out of context and had said that it was a sin to rely on medications. (If that were truly what God meant by this verse, why do we eat food to replenish our bodies?) After a while in this church the woman became convinced that if she had enough faith, God would correct her imbalance and she would not need her medication.

When she quit her medication, the self-critical voices came back, and came back even stronger, because she felt they were caused by her lack of faith, that God had not healed what had been passed down to her genetically. She eventually committed suicide because of her deep anguish and feelings of being rejected already by God. The church that this woman attended now embraces an openness to medication and encourages their members to consider it when needed. Many lives are now changed for the better through this church. It is tragic that this young woman's life had to be lost for us to learn a needed lesson. We included her story here so more lives are not lost as hers was.

A genetic dopamine imbalance results in your thinking that you hear God's audible voice or the audible voice of demons. Taking a dopamine-correcting medicine (like Seroquel) makes these voices disappear. It is important that we do not automatically think that this is purely a spiritual problem. Without the correct medication some people will hear voices in their head that tell them to jump off a building, and they will jump, because they think it is God or they think that they are not worthy of life because the "demon" voices are telling them that. One time on my (Paul's) psychiatry unit I had three patients in group therapy arguing with each other because they all thought they were Jesus, until the medication corrected their dopamine imbalances!

Around 5 percent of the population has a disorder that is primarily genetic, called social phobia, resulting in fear of people, fear of crowds, fear of intimacy, fear of public speaking, fear of sitting in the middle of a row of people, and so on. A majority of those with social phobia abuse drugs or alcohol to self-medicate. (They feel more social or "socially normal" with the drugs or alcohol.) Some people with social phobias can recover by applying the tools they have learned in this book alone or by applying these tools along with therapy. But many will never be able to significantly improve until they take a lifelong medication of either a serotonin medicine (like Effexor-XR, Zoloft, or Celexa) or a GABA medicine (like Topamax, Neurontin, or Depakote-ER). You would be amazed if you were with us during the follow-up visits of people who had suffered with social phobia their whole lives—and thought it was their fault. After three days on Neurontin, for example, one man's whole demeanor and way of being was chemically and biologically balanced. His constant fear of people—which he had experienced all his life—was no longer present to block him. We do not know all the reasons God made our brains so sensitive to imbalance, yet we do know he wants us to love and be loved as this man was given the opportunity to more fully do.

Another 5 percent of the population inherits either attention deficit hyperactivity disorder (ADHD) or a genetic cousin, bipolar disorder. ADHD without medication may keep a person too impulsive to accomplish a deep and responsible relationship with God. A norepinephrine medicine (like Wellbutrin-SR) or a stimulant (like time-released Ritalin) will work to correct ADHD.

Bipolar disorders cause people to have dramatic mood swings from deep depressions to elation and grandiosity, hyperactivity, racing thoughts, and insomnia. Some even become so grandiose that they start their own religious denomination and think that God told them to do so. Others give away their life savings and children's inheritance to a religious-sounding con man. These people can live normal lives and develop a normal and stable relationship with God, self, and others only if they

230

take lifelong medication with a mood stabilizer (like Topamax, Depakote-ER, or Seroquel).

Some people are born with lower serotonin levels in their brain than normal, and this creates depression. In elderly people we sometimes mistake depression for Alzheimer's disease, because with depression some may have symptoms such as forgetfulness, flattened emotions, and irritability.

We encourage you to take care of any imbalances in your brain chemistry and to let go of feeling ashamed of taking care of yourself in this way. Just as we love our children when they feel ashamed for having braces or wearing glasses, it is important for us to show this same kindness to ourselves and others in our lives who have genetic imbalances to correct.

## A Natural Progression

We truly appreciate your joining us on the journey toward learning what it is to form unbreakable bonds and experiencing what it is to love and be loved. In twelve chapters we have shared with you real ways you can begin to conceptualize and reform your ideas of love, as well as concrete ways you can begin to change your experience of love in your own life.

In this closing chapter, in addition to the above biological information, we wish to reveal to you a beautiful coincidence we found after writing the first twelve chapters. We discovered a parallel between the Lord's Prayer and the four sections we created in this book. When we decided on the four main parts of the book, we thought about the natural progression of forming unbreakable bonds. We came up with direction, detection, connection, and perfection. In part 1, chapters 1–4, you determined your *direction*. You essentially asked yourself: Do I want to be loved? Do I deserve to be loved? Where does this love come from? Was I created to love? In part 2, chapters 5–7, you *detected* the ways you were unintentionally blocking love out of your life—by staying in a cave, by allowing yourself to be treated like a doormat, or by holding on to expectations and grudges. In part 3, chapters 8–10, you learned to *connect* by letting go of the grudges, letting go of the blocks that have kept you from love, learning what it is to practice loving God, others, and yourself, and learning how to protect yourself and let go of anger. In the final part, chapters 11–13, you have been working on *perfecting* your ability to love by unifying yourself with God, the perfect source of love, and inviting his love to love you to maturity.

Here, in the Lord's Prayer, we discovered there is a natural progression of spiritual growth that follows a similar course. We invite you to take a few minutes to read and meditate on the mystery of the Lord's Prayer:

> Our Father in heaven,
> Hallowed be Your name.
> Your kingdom come.
> Your will be done
> On earth as it is in heaven.
> Give us this day our daily bread.
> And forgive us our debts,
> As we forgive our debtors.
> And do not lead us into temptation,
> But deliver us from the evil one.
> For Yours is the kingdom and the power and the glory forever.
>     Amen.

Matthew 6:9–13

When Jesus gave us this prayer two thousand years ago, he was not speaking with empty words. These words are a mystery, a powerful mystery. There is a reason these words are repeated daily by Catholics and Protestants the world around as they wake each day. This "Christian" prayer has deep Jewish undertones as well, which you can discover, if you wish, in the final exercise of this chapter.

We invite you to take the time here to consider how this prayer can direct you even more in your process of growth. Consider how we get our *direction* from our Father, the Father and Creator of us all, who loves perfectly. We have the ability to consciously invite the love of God that orders heaven to direct us in our daily life. Consider how we *detect* the emptiness or lack of love in various parts of our own life and ask for God to fill us with both our daily bread (necessities) and the bread of himself to daily feed our souls, restore our perspective, and nourish our spiritual being.

Consider how, in order to *connect* with God and connect with ourselves, it is vital that we take time to detect the unloving ways of being in our lives (our debts). We can then freely ask God to forgive us completely of our debts with his limitless love.

To *connect* with others (and in some ways with God and ourselves), it is important that we take time to detect the grudges we hold against others, which have kept us stuck in a place of anger—where love has little room to enter. Take a moment, open your hands to release your grudges before God, asking him to teach you and work within your heart to reveal to you his love so that you can forgive others as God forgives you.

In order to *perfect* or mature your ability to form unbreakable bonds, ask God to lead you toward his love, to reveal his presence to your heart, to show you his love and ground you in it so that temptation to take shortcuts or twist the good will not even be tempting to you! Ask God to deliver you from your weaknesses and teach you how to be aware of them—and coach them toward unifying with your soul's deeper purpose of holiness. God is our perfect source of love, and in him is all truth. Perfect your ability to form unbreakable bonds by learning how to humbly walk with your loving Father, recognizing that we are walking toward his kingdom of love with his power, which works in us to love for his glory, not because he needs us to glorify him but because he is a beautiful Creator. We are made in his image, creating love in our own unique way, reflecting him. He is the Creator over all who fills us with love that we may give it to others. We were made to connect with him and glorify him, for in doing this we glorify the giver of love.

*Amen* is the wrapping-up part of the prayer. *Amen* means "Let it be done." Remember that *perfection* means to do thoroughly, or to be done thoroughly. We wish you love as you invite the love of God to fill your whole being thoroughly, through and through, as you continue practicing the art of loving and being loved. As you invite his love to help you apply the principles of this book to your own life, remember to share this love with others and give it back to God. Pray for others who do not yet know this deep love or do not yet recognize where they can find it.

May God truly bless you and love your heart.

## The Lord's Prayer Exercise

Take time to understand the Jewish roots of the Lord's Prayer and write down other insights you find from reading these Scriptures and praying the Lord's Prayer.

There is an age-old Jewish tradition derived from one of God's commandments in Deuteronomy. In this tradition, as the Jewish infant enters the world, in the first moments of his or her life the Sh'ma text is whispered in his ear: "Hear, O Israel: The LORD our God, the LORD is one. Love the LORD your God with all your heart and with all your soul and with all your strength" (6:4–5 NIV).

Our Father in heaven,
Hallowed be Your name.

As the Jewish child grows up into the faith, he or she is taught to study the Torah, the Law of God, and to follow it.

Your will be done on earth as it is in heaven.

When we observe the history of the Jewish people, we see how they were led out of slavery into the Promised Land of Israel. During their wanderings and their journey to this Promised Land, God provided them each day with bread from the sky called manna. *Manna* is translated: "We do not know what" or "What is it?" They literally did not know what to call this mysterious bread provided daily to them from heaven.

Give us this day our daily bread.

When the Israelites tried to gather more than a day's worth of bread, it became covered with maggots and was inedible. However, on Fridays they were able to gather enough for two days, and it was edible on the next day, the Sabbath. This meant that they could rest and not gather on the Lord's Day.

Jesus was called "the bread of heaven." He was born, in fact, in Bethlehem, which literally means "the house of bread." When we have communion, we repeat the words that Jesus said before his crucifixion: "Take this bread, which is my body, broken for you. Do this in remembrance of me."

The Israelites were given this in the Torah: "So the priest shall make atonement for him before the LORD, and he shall be forgiven for any one of these things that he may have done in which he trespasses" (Lev. 6:7).

And forgive us our debts,

> You shall not hate your brother in your heart. You shall surely rebuke your neighbor, and not bear sin because of him. You shall not take vengeance, nor bear any grudge against the children of your people, but you shall love your neighbor as yourself: I am the LORD.
>
> Leviticus 19:17–18

As we forgive our debtors.

We read in the Psalms, the words of King David:

> He restores my soul;
> He leads me in the paths of righteousness
> For His name's sake.
> Yea, though I walk through the valley of the shadow of death,
> I will fear no evil;
> For You are with me.
>
> Psalm 23:3–4

And do not lead us into temptation,
But deliver us from the evil one.

Show me Your ways, O Lord;
Teach me Your paths.
Lead me in Your truth and teach me,
For You are the God of my salvation.

Psalm 25:4–5

For Yours is the kingdom and the power and the glory forever.

We see, then, that the prayer Jesus taught his disciples two thousand years ago is rooted in Old Testament texts, written more than two thousand years before Christ. As we meditate on this prayer daily and allow it to take root in our lives, we discover the foundations of truth with which God created the world.

The Lord by wisdom founded the earth;
By understanding He established the heavens. . . .
My son, let them not depart from your eyes—
Keep sound wisdom and discretion;
So they will be life to your soul
And grace to your neck.
Then you will walk safely in your way,
And your foot will not stumble.
When you lie down, you will not be afraid;
Yes, you will lie down and your sleep will be sweet. . . .
For the Lord will be your confidence,
And will keep your foot from being caught.

Proverbs 3:19, 21–24, 26

We discover, as we live out this prayer, restoration for our souls and connection with God, ourselves, and one another.

# Notes

## Introduction

1. David G. Benner, *Psychotherapy and the Spiritual Quest* (Grand Rapids: Baker, 1988), 51.

2. Mother Teresa, *No Greater Love* (Novato, Calif.: New World Library, 1997), 53.

## Chapter 2 Creating a Path to Love

1. J. R. R. Tolkien, in *Essays Presented to Charles Williams* (New York: Oxford University Press, 1947), 74.

2. Jay P. Green, ed., *The Interlinear Bible: Hebrew-Greek-English* (Peabody, Mass.: Hendrickson Publishers, 1986).

3. This is also reflected in a verse in Romans: "For since the creation of the world God's invisible qualities—his eternal power and divine nature—have been clearly seen, being understood from what has been made" (Rom. 1:20 NIV). See also Psalm 19:1–6.

4. It is really an infinite amount. One hundred percent cannot begin to capture the amount of love available to us, yet we use one hundred percent here to try to grasp the concept.

5. This idea was presented to Cheryl years ago by a professor at Talbot Seminary and Biola University, Dr. Jerry Root.

6. A verse in the GNB (Good News Bible) speaks to this: "Discipline your children while they are young enough to learn. If you don't, you are helping them destroy themselves" (Prov. 19:18).

7. G. K. Chesterton, *Orthodoxy* (1908; reprint, Westport, Conn.: Greenwood Press, 1974), 43.

## Chapter 3 Re-membering Yourself

1. Cheryl Meier, "Review of Empirical Literature Regarding Formation of God Concept and the Relationship of Father Involvement" (Ph.D. diss., Rosemead Graduate School of Psychology, 1999).

2. "Damascus," archeological supplement in *Thompson Chain-Reference Bible*, ed. Frank Charles Thompson (1910; reprint, Indianapolis: B. B. Kirkbride Bible Co., 1988), 1785.

## Chapter 4 Determining Your Direction

1. J. P. Green Sr., *The Greek/English Pocket Interlinear New Testament* (Grand Rapids: Baker, 1991).

2. Adin Steinsaltz, *The Thirteen Petalled Rose: A Discourse of Jewish Existence and Belief* trans. Yehuda Haneghi (Basic Books, 1980), 69.

3. George MacDonald, *Unspoken Sermons* (Los Angeles: J. Joseph Flynn, 1988). All of George MacDonald's works are available free on e-text at www.johannesen.com

4. Rabbi Nosson Scherman, *The Stone Edition: The Torah, Haftaros and Five Megillos with a Commentary Anthologized from the Rabbinic Writings* (Brooklyn, N.Y.: Mesorah Publications, 1994), 555.

5. Mother Teresa, One Heart Full of Love, ed. Jose Luis Gonzalez-Balado (Ann Arbor, Mich.: Servant Books, 1988), 129.

## Chapter 6 Am I a Doormat?

1. Green, *Pocket Interlinear New Testament;* also found in Deuteronomy 32:35–36.

2. George MacDonald, *The Princess and the Goblin* (New York: HarperFestival, 2002).

3. Rainer Maria Rilke, *Letters to a Young Poet,* trans. Stephen Mitchell (New York: Random House, 1984), 92.

## Chapter 7 What Do You Expect?

1. Leo Tolstoy, in *Calendar of Wisdom: Daily Thoughts to Nourish the Soul,* trans. Peter Sekirin (New York: Scribner, 1997), 153 (May 20).

2. C. S. Lewis, *The Four Loves* (Harvest Book, 1960), 158; italics mine.

3. Ibid., 159; italics mine.

4. C. S. Lewis, *The Problem of Pain* (New York: Macmillan, 1944).

## Chapter 8 Preparing for Limitless Love

1. Leo Tolstoy, *Calendar of Wisdom,* 67.

2. Aristotle, *Nichomachean Ethics,* book II, chapter 1.

3. George MacDonald *Lilith:* A Romance by George MacDonald (1895; reprint, Grand Rapids: Eerdmans, 1981), 218.

4. Mother Teresa, *A Simple Path,* comp. Lucinda Vardey (New York: Ballantine, 1995), 185.

## Chapter 9 Practicing the Art of Love

1. Lewis, *The Problem of Pain,* 38.

## Chapter 11 Changing the Way I Treat Myself

1. I was training pastors about psychology and psychiatry so they could better minister to the people in their churches.

2. Boundaries books are published by Zondervan: Henry Cloud and John Townsend, *Boundaries: When to Say Yes, When to Say No to Take Control of Your Life* (1992), *Boundaries in Marriage* (1999), *Boundaries in Dating* (2000), *Boundaries with Kids* (2001).

3. Mother Teresa, *No Greater Love,* 14.

4. This is what Jesus said the role of the Holy Spirit is in John 14:26—our comforter or helper.

5. Leo Tolstoy, *Calendar of Wisdom.*

## Chapter 12 Creating an Unbreakable Bond with God

1. Saint Augustine wrote, "Our hearts are restless until they find their rest in Thee [God]."

2. Boethius, *The Consolation of Philosophy*, trans. V. E. Watts (Baltimore: Penguin, 1969), 79.

3. From the *Basic English Bible.*

4. Mother Teresa, *No Greater Love*, 53, 57, 63.

5. Søren Kierkegaard, *Either/Or II* (Princeton, N.J.: Princeton University Press, 1987), 203, 220. The passage of Scripture he quotes are the words of Jesus from Matthew 16:26.

6. C. S. Lewis, *The Weight of Glory* (New York: Macmillan, 1949), 2.

7. See Isaiah 7:14 and Matthew 1:23. *Immanuel* means "God with us." See also John 1:14.

**Dr. Cheryl Meier** received her doctorate in Clinical Psychology from Rosemead School of Psychology. She is the clinical director of the San Juan Capistrano Meier Clinic in Southern California and the cohost of two radio shows that focus on educating the public on psychological topics such as depression, perfectionism, anxiety, and eating disorders.

**Dr. Paul Meier** is a nationally recognized psychiatrist and the founder of Meier Clinics, with over thirty clinic programs located throughout the country. He is a radio cohost on *Consumer* magazine with Pete Thompson of KWRD in Dallas, Texas, and is an internationally sought after speaker. He is the coauthor of *Happiness Is a Choice* and over fifty other books. Dr. Meier is also the founding member of the Physician Advisory Council of Focus on the Family. He practices psychiatry at the Meier Clinics in Richardson, Texas. To reach the nearest Meier Clinic, call 1-888-7CLINIC (1-888-725-4642) or check them out on the web at www.meierclinics.com.